The Power of Peter, the Fisherman, and Mary, the Magdalene

JAMES O. PELLICER

The Power of Peter, the Fisherman, and Mary, the Magdalene

The biblical texts quoted in this study are taken from Novi Testamenti Biblia Graeca et Latina, a work prepared by Professor José M. Bover S.J. from the School of Theology and Consultant of the Pontifical Commission on Biblical Matters, Madrid, and published by the Consejo Superior de Investigaciones Científicas in 1943. The translation of all biblical texts are by this writer in con-sultation with The Holy Bible - The New Jerusalem Bible, Copyright by American Bible Society, 1992, frequently checking with El Nuevo Testamento según el texto original griego, translated and commented by Mons. Dr. Juan Straubinger, published in 1948 by Dedebec, Ediciones Desclée de Brouwer, Buenos Aires.

iUniverse books may be ordered through booksellers or by contacting:

iUniverse
1663 Liberty Drive
Bloomington, IN 47403
www.iuniverse.com
1-800-Authors (1-800-288-4677)

ISBN: 978-1-5320-2771-0 (sc)
ISBN: 978-1-5320-2773-4 (hc)
ISBN: 978-1-5320-2772-7 (e)

Library of Congress Control Number: 2017912504

Print information available on the last page.

iUniverse rev. date: 10/27/2017

Contents

FIRST PART

Introduction

The present work is dedicated to two characters of the early Christian days and is divided in two parts: 1) The analysis of the Apostle Peter's power and 2) The character and personality of Mary Magdalene. She will be seen as the representative of all women whose total exclusion from the ministry and Church administration up to the present day will be also considered.

All possible sources of historical evidence will be used in order to scientifically establish the theme. This study is then a historical inquiry regarding the hypothetical power of the Apostle Peter, claimed as well by his hypothetical successors who consider themselves sole representatives of Jesus Christ on earth with the title of "Pontifex Maximus." At the same time, the importance of Mary Magdalene from the point of view of Jesus Christ will also be studied with a complete exclusion of all legends which surround her name.

Although this subject touches upon another very important theme, the religious one, this monograph has nothing to do with matters belonging to the domain of religion nor is the intention of its author to make affirmations or negations within such a theme.

In order to arrive at the definition of the "power of Peter", earliest documents in which this name appears will be examined: first, the New Testament and other gospels from the earliest days of Christianity, which have been progressively discovered since the end of the Nineteenth Century. Finally, the early writers of Christianity will be reviewed.

The same steps will be taken to examine Mary Magdalene's mission and demission. She will be seen as the representative of women. It is necessary to include her in this study on Peter since he called her "insane" when she went to the apostles with the information of the Lord's resurrection, and -in addition- he is quoted as declaring all women "not worthy of life" (as a matter of fact, all women continue to be excluded from ministry and leadership positions in the Roman Catholic Church) and despite that the resurrected Jesus made her the apostle to the apostles, the Roman Papacy declared her a prostitute ... repentant .. of course.

Conclusions and corollaries will close the study before the bibliography which will offer the reader an extended field where to satisfy his/her scientific curiosity.

Explanation of terms

"Pontifex Maximus" refers to the head of the "Roman Catholic Church", although its leaders prefer omitting the word "Roman" because they consider it restrictive since "catholic" means "universal", "total"; from Latin "catholicus" which comes from old Greek "katholikós", a word formed by two pieces: "katá" (in reference to) and "holos" (the whole, total, in reference to totality). In addition, the word "pontifex" = pontiff is formed by two Latin parts: 1) Pont = bridge and 2) fex = maker. One who makes the bridge between God and people. "Maximus" is the superlative for great, the greatest creator of the bridge between God and humans.

The said organization declares that it is the one and only assembly that legitimately congregate all of those who profess Christianity. Nevertheless, there are many churches which proclaim themselves "catholic". In addition to the Roman, we have the Greek Orthodox, the Russian, the Anglican, the Scottish, the Sirio-Lebanese, the Episcopal; i.e. the churches which accept the Creed proclaimed in Nicaea in the year 325.

The word "power" derives from low Latin "potere" which comes from classic Latin "posse" and refers to the extent to which someone or something may reach.

After having explained all terms, it is possible to define the "power" proclaimed by the Roman Pontiff: this power is total. The Pontiff definitely declares that he is the only legitimate representative of God and, as such, his domain includes all reality, either present or future. In addition, he cannot be wrong when he speaks in his capacity of official head of the church; in other words, he is infallible. The terms he uses to declare this tenet is "pontifical infallibility" when he speaks "ex cathedra", i.e. from the chair; this is to say, as God's representative he cannot say something erroneous; he cannot make a mistake. For this reason, this pontiff has proclaimed canons so absolute as the following: "*It is totally unacceptable to appeal a sentence or a decree from the Roman Pontiff*" (Canon 333.3).

The biblical texts quoted in this study are taken from *Novi Testamenti Biblia Graeca et Latina*, prepared by Prof. José M. Bover S.J., consultant of the Pontifical Commission on Biblical Matters, Madrid, and published by the Consejo de Investigaciones Científicas in 1943. The translation of all biblical texts are by this writer in consultation with *The Holy Bible - The New Jerusalem Bible*, Copyright by American Bible Society, 1992, frequently checking with *El Nuevo Testamento según el texto original griego,* translated into Spanish and commented by Mons. Dr. Juan Straubinger, published in 1948 by Dedebec, Ediciones Desclée de Brouwer, Buenos Aires. Another Spanish translation which has been kept at hand is *La Santa Biblia --- Antiguo y Nuevo Testamento. Antigua Versión de Casiodoro de Reina (1569), Revisada por Cipriano de Valera (1602), Revisión de 1960,* Published by Sociedades Bíblicas en América Latina. Also a French text has been consulted: *La Sainte Bible qui comprend l'Ancien et le Nouveau Testament traduits sur les textes originaux Hebreu et Grec, par Louis Segond, docteur en Théologie. Paris, 1966.* Finally, in order to avoid any possible problem due to religious affiliation, another work has been frequently consulted: *The Protestant- Roman Catholic New Testament. Revised Standard Version --- Confraternity Version. The Iversen-Ford Associates, New York, 1964.*

Chapter I

The Origin of the Name "Peter"

The word "peter" as such does not show up in any original text. It was brought into England by the Normans as "Pier". Later it acquired the form of "Peter" and was used to interpret the name Jesus gave to Simon, one of his disciples; "Kefas", in Aramaic. The first Greek translation gave it as "Petros" which translates into English as "stone" as it appears in the Gospel of Mark, which the scholars date as written by the end of the sixties or beginning of the seventies. There are no original texts.[1] Its author is unknown although an old tradition attributes it to a man named "Marcus", also unknown. It narrates the life of Jesus of Nazareth from his baptism by John the Baptist until his resurrection and ascension into Heaven.

The text in question reads as follows:

> *He now went up onto the mountain and summoned those He wanted. So they came to Him. And He appointed twelve; they were to be His companions and to be sent out to proclaim the message with power to drive out devils. And so He appointed the Twelve, Simon to whom He gave the name Peter (πετρον = petron = stone) James the son of Zebedee and John, the brother of James, to whom*

---

[1] Codex Sinaiticus is the oldest known text of the New Testament. It was discovered by Friedrich Constantin von Tischendorf in 1844 in the Monastery of Santa Catalina in the Sinai Mountain. It was originally written between the years 330 and 350. It is now in the British Library, London.

> *He gave the name Boanerges or "Sons of Thunder".* etc.
> (Mark 3:13-17)

This short text has started a gigantic production of studies on the nicknames given by Jesus, mainly "stone" applied to Simon. We do not know why Jesus used nicknames for his disciples. The one which is of concern here is "stone" given to Simon.

A few lines before, the Gospel of Mark had stated: *"As He was walking along by the Lake of Galilee, He saw Simon and Simon's brother Andrew casting a net in the lake - for they were fishermen."* (Mark 1:16) This is the first time Simon appears in history although without the attached word "stone" which is mentioned a few paragraphs thereafter as seen in the previous quotation.

The Gospel of Matthew directly begins with the name "stone" applied to Simon:

> *As He was walking by the Lake of Galilee, He saw two brothers, Simon who was called Peter (πετρον=stone) and his brother Andrew* (Matthew 4:15).

The Gospel of Luke also mentions Simon, first without any attachment and thereafter with the word "stone" applied to him, as follows:

> *One day as Jesus was standing by the Lake of Gennesaret, the people were crowding around him and listening to the word of God.* ^{2} *He saw at the water's edge two boats, left there by the fishermen, who were washing their nets.* ^{3} *He got into one of the boats, the one belonging to Simon, and asked him to put out a little from shore. Then he sat down and taught the people from the boat.* ^{4} *When he had finished speaking, he said to Simon, "Put out into deep water, and let down the nets for a catch.* ^{5} *Simon answered, "Master, we worked hard all night and haven't caught anything, but because you say so, I will let down the*

nets." *⁶ When they had done so, they caught such a large number of fish that their nets began to break. ⁷ So they signaled their partners in the other boat to come and help them, and they came and filled both boats so full that they began to sink. ⁸ When Simon Peter saw this, he fell at Jesus' knees and said, "Go away from me, Lord; I am a sinful man!". ⁹ For he and all his companions were astonished at the catch of fish they had taken, ¹⁰ and so were James and John, the sons of Zebedee, Simon's partners. Then Jesus said to Simon, "Don't be afraid; from now on you will fish for people." ¹¹ So they pulled their boats up on shore, left everything and followed him.* (Luke 5: 1-11)

The Gospel of John is the only one which employs the original term used by Jesus in His Aramaic language, *"Kefas"*. The word appears as referred to Simon, the brother of Andrew who was interested in the lectures of a Jewish ascetic preacher named John, the Baptist. According to this gospel, John was near the Jordan River with his disciples when Jesus passed by. John stared at Jesus and said aloud: *"Behold the Lamb of God!"*. Upon hearing this, Andrew with another unnamed disciple left John and followed Jesus who, upon realizing that he was followed, turned around and asked them what they were looking for. They answered with another question: *"Where do you live?"* Jesus replied: *"Come and see it"*. They then followed Him, checked the place, and looked for a site to stay because it was already late. Then, Andrew went to find his brother Simon and told him: *"we have found the Messiah!"* and brought him to Jesus who greeted him with the following words: *"You are Simon, the son of John; you will be called Kefas* (which translates as "stone") (πετρος) (Jn 1:42).

None of the gospels gives a reason for the name "stone" and only Mark and John inform us that Jesus was the one who gave him such a name.

The word used by Jesus was *"kefas"* which, translated from Aramaic and other Semitic languages, refers to a small green stone used by sorcerers and magicians in order to see or discover some hidden reality. Perhaps this may refer to another moment in the communications between Jesus and Peter when according to the Gospel of Matthew Jesus asked his disciples *"Who do people say that the Son of Man is?"* (...) Simon Peter answered, *"You are the Messiah, the Son of the living God."* (Mat. 16:13-16) Jesus, then, congratulated Peter because such a revelation of a hidden reality was not due to a human skill.

Until this point we have studied the incoming into history of a character named "Simon", a name which comes from the Greek language of the New Testament as Σιμων (Simon), which at the same time is a translation from Hebrew שמעון (Shimon) which means "God has heard".

Chapter II

Peter in the Four Canonical Gospels

In this chapter, we shall present only those passages from the Gospels in which Peter (or Simon) is directly mentioned without considering the ones which refer to the disciples in general, with one exception which will be precisely indicated.

The word "gospel" connotes an early narration on the life and sayings of Jesus Christ. The word comes from Old English: godspel, literally "good spell," from "good" (adj.) + spel "story, message". In other words, glad tidings announced by Jesus. These glad tidings were that God had offered hope and redemption for the human race.

In the last few years, several of the lost writings were found and catalogued as "apocryphal" (hidden) or "Gnostic gospels" (from the knowledge). The canonic gospels, on the contrary, are the four which succeeded in this long struggle for recognition. These gospels were controlled by the proto-orthodox and their writers were called "Matthew", "Mark", "Luke", and "John" despite the fact that these four had nothing to do with the true writers who perhaps never even knew Jesus and His land.

St. Irenaeus, a bishop from the last days of the second century, born in what is Turkey today, was the champion of those four gospels and the group of the proto-orthodox itself. His fundamental belief was that truth resides in the total union and agreement with the bishop. This tenet generated a solid vertical and compact group, better equipped to succeed in the initial struggles of Christianity vis a vis the divided groups called "heretic" which had maintained themselves faithful to Jesus' mandate of not imposing themselves on the others and respected the simple equality of the first disciples. The hierarchic group succeeded and the others disappeared through time and persecutions.

No one knows when the canonical gospels were written or by whom; nevertheless for the sake of understanding the names of the traditional evangelists will be maintained: Matthew, Mark, Luke, and John. These gospels were written in Greek, a language totally strange to the Jews, mainly for the poor fishermen, disciples of Jesus. The Bible itself testifies that Peter and John were illiterate (Acts 4:13). Certainly, Jesus' disciples were not men of letters or experts in foreign languages.

Regarding the dates, some scholars affirm that the gospels of Matthew (year 85) and Luke (year 90) derive from Mark, written around the year 70, and other text now lost, called "Q" (from German, "quelle" = "source". The last of the gospels, that of John, could have been written between 95 and 100. There are no original texts; the most ancient copies which we have were written in Greek around the Fourth Century, discovered in the Nineteenth, by the German researcher Constantin von Tischendorf in a monastery located in Mount Sinai from which we have the name of "Codex Sinaiticus"

1. **The Gospel of Saint Matthew:**

The Gospel According to Matthew (<u>Greek</u>: κατὰ Ματθαῖον εὐαγγέλιον)is one of the four <u>canonical gospels</u>, one of the three <u>synoptic gospels</u>, and the first book of the <u>New Testament</u>. The narrative tells how the <u>Messiah</u>, <u>Jesus</u>, <u>rejected by Israel</u>, finally <u>sends the disciples</u> to preach his Gospel to the whole world. Most scholars believe the Gospel of Matthew was composed between 80 and 90 CE.

Peter appears in fifteen occasions, some of them as Simon and some others as Simon Peter (Stone), or simply Peter (Stone). Immediately, the passages in which the Apostle appears mentioned by name will be transcribed, except the last one in which he is included under the term "disciples".

1) **Matthew 4: 18-20:** *As Jesus was walking beside the Sea of Galilee, he saw two brothers, Simon called Peter and his brother Andrew. They were casting a net into the lake, for they were fishermen. "Come, follow me," Jesus said, "and I will send you out to fish for people." At once they left their nets and followed him.* This is the first time in which this character appears in the Gospel of Matthew although not in history because the Gospel of Mark was written earlier.

2) **Matthew 8: 14-15:** *When Jesus came into Peter's house, he saw Peter's mother-in-law lying in bed with a fever. He touched her hand and the fever left her, and she got up and began to wait on him.* The Greek text textually says: "oikian Petrou" (in the Peter's house). This mention is rather indirect but it is useful to locate Peter in a precise place. Jesus had arrived in Capernaum (a town on the northwest coast of the Sea of Galilee, where he had cured a servant of the Centurion in the service of King Herod Antipas, the Tetrarch of Galilee. There was the house in which Peter, his wife and his mother in law lived together. If they had children, it is impossible to know it, although one of the Gnostic Gospels mentions a daughter.

3) **Matthew 10: 2-3:** *These are the names of the twelve apostles: first, Simon (who is called Peter) and his brother Andrew; James son of Zebedee, and his brother John; Philip and Bartholomew; Thomas and Matthew the tax collector; James son of Alphaeus, and Thaddaeus; Simon the Zealot and Judas Iscariot, who betrayed him.* Reference to Peter, is first, in the list of the twelve names.

4) **Matthew 14: 28-32:** *"Lord, if it's you," Peter replied, "tell me to come to you on the water." "Come," he said. Then Peter got down out of the boat, walked on the water and came toward Jesus. But when he saw the wind, he was afraid and, beginning to sink, cried out, "Lord, save me! Immediately Jesus reached out his hand and caught him. "You of little faith," he said, "why did you doubt?" And*

when they climbed into the boat, the wind died down. This text narrates that Jesus had appeared to his fishermen disciples walking on the waters and had approached Peter's boat. The disciples were terrorized believing that He was a ghost. Jesus identified himself and calmed them down. Peter conditioned his believe in Jesus to a capacity of walking on the water.

5) **Matthew 15:15:** *Peter said, "Explain the parable to us."* At Peter's request, Jesus refers to whatever enters and comes out from people. That what comes out is what really defiles a person: murder, adultery, sexual immorality, theft, false testimony, slander.

6) **Matthew 16: 13-19:** *[3] When Jesus came to the region of Caesarea Philippi, he asked his disciples, "Who do people say the Son of Man is?" They replied, "Some say John the Baptist; others say Elijah; and still others, Jeremiah or one of the prophets." "But what about you?" he asked. "Who do you say I am? "Simon Peter answered, "You are the Messiah, the Son of the living God." Jesus replied, "Blessed are you, Simon son of Jonah, for this was not revealed to you by flesh and blood, but by my Father in heaven.* **And I tell you that you are Peter and on this rock I will build my church, and the gates of Hades will not overcome it. I will give you the keys of the kingdom of heaven; whatever you bind on earth will be bound in heaven, and whatever you loose on earth will be loosed in heaven."** (verses 18 and 19).

In this evangelical passage appears **the most famous mention of Peter**.

The text is very strange because Jesus never said that He would found or build churches or any other type of organization but just the contrary, that everything was ending because the Kingdom of God was coming.

It is also important to keep in mind the discussion the apostles had a short time afterwards about whom among them would be greater in the Kingdom. Jesus' simple answer was to put a child in the center (Matthew 18: 1-5). It was obvious: no one was more important than the others. This reaction of Jesus openly and directly contradicts the supposed Peter's appointment for a "Primacy". All the other gospels conclude the so called "Peter's confession" with the prohibition by Jesus of revealing that He was the Christ. Nothing else. Nothing else!!! There are no keys to any kingdom, or tying/untying anything, even less of building a church. And worst of all, building on a human being as the foundation stone, precisely in this case long before prophesied by Isaiah in the sense that the foundation stone was the Christ! Obviously, this text is a later interpolation and worst of all, blasphemous! with political intentions as we shall see later.

Notice in addition that this text implicitly affirms that there is only one church as one Empire with only one absolute monarch from which all other groups would depend like the dioceses of the Roman Empire. Obviously, the Roman Imperial mentality is behind it. Nevertheless, the Christian reality was not like that; the churches created by Saint Paul do not appear as subjects of any other church or dependent from a higher institution. Furthermore, the later churches of Greece or Russia or Lebanon never appeared as subordinates or their bishops dependent on other more powerful prelates, even less from a Roman bishop.

By the way, the scholars who admit this text as authentic make extraordinary efforts to explain that Jesus used the word "petros" (little pebble) to refer to Simon and right after "rock" to mean Himself. These scholars do not realize that such an interpretation sounds like a joke or worse, an insult that Jesus addresses to Peter. Nevertheless, Jesus' intention was not correcting Peter but praising him because the very same Celestial Father had revealed to Peter that He -Jesus- was the Christ.

Instead of explaining this text, it is preferable to simply admit that the text is a later insertion made by a Romanist who did not realize the incongruence of what he was doing or could not care less.

On the other hand, the expression attributed to Jesus: "I will build my "ecclesia", the word "ecclesia" (English, "church" and Greek "εκκλεσια" = "ecclesia") is out of context and reveals a much later date. In the days of Jesus, "ecclesia" meant an aristocratic Greek, pagan organization of Athenian youth, sons of Athenian parents, who went on a pilgrimage forty times a year to Mount Knyx in the center of Athens. Jesus could not know it and even less say such a word as something very well known and His listeners understand it. Even less acceptable is that Jesus was talking about building or founding a pagan organization and even less, proposing it as an example. This word took many years to enter the Christian vocabulary, just when Christianity was extending into the Greek world.

Obviously, this text is an interpolation added when Rome was beginning to impose itself on the rest of Christianity. It did it at the expense of Peter, as we shall see later.

7) **Matthew 16: 22-23:** *Peter took him aside and began to rebuke him. "Never, Lord!" he said. "This shall never happen to you!" Jesus turned and said to Peter, "Get behind me, Satan! You are a stumbling block to me; you do not have in mind the concerns of God, but merely human concerns."* Jesus had announced his sufferings and death. As it is obvious, this text after the previous one, presents another contradiction: Peter is not the "First" Christian bishop but "Satan".

8) **Matthew 17: 1-6:** *And after six days Jesus taketh Peter, James, and John his brother, and bringeth them up into a high mountain apart. And was transfigured before them: and his face did shine as the sun, and his raiment was white as the light. And, behold, there appeared unto them Moses and Elias talking with him. Then answered Peter, and said unto Jesus, Lord, it is good for us to be here: if thou wilt, let us make here three tabernacles; one for thee, and one for Moses, and one for Elias. While he yet spake, behold, a bright cloud overshadowed them: and behold a voice out of the cloud, which said, This is my beloved Son, in whom I am well pleased; hear ye him.[6] And when the disciples heard it, they fell on their face, and were sore afraid.* This passage is known as "the transfiguration of the Lord". Peter appears as saying one of his famous foolish commentaries.

9) **Matthew 17: 24.27:** *After Jesus and his disciples arrived in Capernaum, the collectors of the two-drachma temple tax came to Peter and asked, "Doesn't your teacher pay the temple tax?" (…)* Jesus said: *"But so that we may not cause offense, go to the lake and throw out your line. Take the first fish you catch; open its mouth and you will find a four-drachma coin. Take it and give it to them for my tax and yours."* The text deals with paying the tribute due to the temple. Jesus had said that the children of God were free but to avoid scandal, they should pay.

10) **Matthew 18: 21-22:** *Then Peter came to Jesus and asked, "Lord, how many times shall I forgive my brother or sister who sins against me? Up to seven times?" Jesus answered, "I tell you, not seven times, but seventy-seven times.* This is the theme of forgiveness. Seven is a symbolic number; it means the perfection of something. In this case, it means "always".

11) **Matthew 19: 27-28:** *Peter answered him, "We have left everything to follow you! What then will there be for us?" Jesus said to them, "Truly I tell you, at the renewal of all things, when the Son of Man sits on his glorious throne, you who have followed me will also sit on twelve thrones, judging the twelve tribes of Israel. And everyone who has left houses or brothers or sisters or father or mother or wife or children or fields for my sake will receive a hundred times as much and will inherit eternal life.* Jesus had spoken on the danger of wealth. "It is easier, He said, that a rope enters through the eye of a needle, than for a rich man to enter into the kingdom of God." Obviously, Peter was making calculations on gains and losses.

12) **Matthew 26: 30-35:** *After singing a hymn, they went out to the Mount of Olives. Then Jesus said to them, "You will all fall away because of Me this night, for it is written, 'I will strike down the shepherd, and the sheep of the flock shall be scattered. But after I have been raised, I will go ahead of you to Galilee." But Peter said to Him, "Even though all may fall away because of You, I will never fall away." Jesus said to him, "Truly I say to you that this very night, before a rooster crows, you will deny Me three times." Peter said to*

Him, "Even if I have to die with You, I will not deny You." All the disciples said the same thing too. This exchange between Jesus and Peter happens right after the last supper in which Jesus predicted the treason of one of the twelve and afterwards gave them the bread and the wine as symbols of His body and blood. Then he finished his speech saying that He would not drink the fruit of the vine again until the day He would do it in the Father's kingdom.

13) **Matthew 26: 36-46**: *Then Jesus went with his disciples to a place called Gethsemane, and he said to them, "Sit here while I go over there and pray." He took Peter and the two sons of Zebedee along with him, and he began to be sorrowful and troubled. (. . .) Then he returned to his disciples and found them sleeping. "Couldn't you men keep watch with me for one hour?" he asked Peter. (. . .)"Rise! Let us go! Here comes my betrayer!"* Three times Jesus went to see his disciples and always they were sleeping. Jesus directs his complaint to Peter.

14) **Matthew 26: 69-75:** *Now Peter was sitting out in the courtyard, and a servant girl came to him. "You also were with Jesus of Galilee," she said. But he denied it before them all. "I don't know what you're talking about," he said. Then he went out to the gateway, where another servant girl saw him and said to the people there, "This fellow was with Jesus of Nazareth." He denied it again, with an oath: "I don't know the man!" After a little while, those standing there went up to Peter and said, "Surely you are one of them; your accent gives you away." Then he began to call down curses, and he swore to them, "I don't know the man!." Immediately a rooster crowed. Then Peter remembered the word Jesus had spoken: "Before the rooster crows, you will disown me three times."* This is the very well known episode of the three times in which Peter repeated the declaration of his apostasy before the rooster's crowing. It seems that Matthew emphasizes the apostasy of Peter by placing him in front of very simple women; thus, his denial resonates more aggravated and he appears more scorned.

15) **Matthew 26:75:** *And he went outside and wept bitterly.* In this text Peter's character does not appear very favorably. Just "cry" and "disappear"? This is the last time Peter is mentioned in this gospel.

Mainly keep in mind that this is the only gospel in which Jesus appears as giving Peter the primacy. Nevertheless, the gospel ends just like that: "he went outside and wept bitterly". Nothing else? The incongruence is more than obvious. This is the conclusion on Peter in this Gospel of Matthew: crying and completely disappearing. It is more than obvious that the affirmation of the primacy, the keys, the building on the rock, the binding and loosening is a very late insertion for very specific reasons. We shall return on to this issue.

16) **Matthew 28: 18-19:** *Then Jesus came to them and said, "All authority in heaven and on earth has been given to me. Therefore, go and make disciples of all nations, baptizing them in the name of the Father and of the Son and of the Holy Spirit, and teaching them to obey everything I have commanded you. And surely I am with you always, to the very end of the age."* After the bitter crying of Peter, this gospel stops mentioning him by name. There is no indication that Jesus had destined Peter to a higher special function within the group or that He could have established any sort of hierarchy among the apostles. All of them, together and in the same manner, had been sent to preach what Jesus had taught them, and above them there was no superior person but Jesus. Even less that the apostles had to receive the confirmation from Peter about what they were to preach. Only Jesus is above them, equally, until the end of the centuries.

2. <u>The Gospel of Saint Mark:</u>

The **Gospel According to Mark** (Greek: τὸ κατὰ Μᾶρκον εὐαγγέλιον, *to kata Markon euangelion*), the second book of the New

Testament, is one of the four canonical gospels, also known as the second synoptic. It was traditionally thought to be a summary of Matthew, which accounts for its place as the second gospel in the Bible, but most contemporary scholars now regard it as the earliest of the gospels.

Most modern scholars reject the tradition which ascribes it to Mark the Evangelist, the companion of Peter, and regard it as the work of an unknown writer although according to an old tradition, it was Mark, a character quoted in some passages of the New Testament, also unknown, who was working with various sources including collections of miracle stories, controversy stories, parables, and a passion narrative.

This is the shortest of the four canonical gospels and also the oldest according to the scholars, who agree in dating it in the last days of the sixties. It begins mentioning St. John the Baptist. Jesus is baptized by John and afterwards retires to the desert for forty days and is tempted by Satan. Upon returning, and near the Sea of Galilee, He started his public life preaching on the streets. His fundamental theme was: "*The time has come. The kingdom of God has come near. Repent and believe the good news!*".

This text proves what we have previously affirmed: Jesus came to the world to announce the final arrival of God's Kingdom; not to found anything and even less to establish a church.

1) **Mark 1: 16-18:** *As Jesus walked beside the Sea of Galilee, he saw Simon and his brother Andrew casting a net into the lake, for they were fishermen. "Come, follow me," Jesus said, "and I will send you out to fish for people." At once they left their nets and followed him.* This is the first time Peter appears in this gospel but under his own name of Simon. He is fishing with nets. He obeys Jesus' call, leaves his nets and follows Him.

2) **Mark 1: 29-31:** *As soon as they left the synagogue, they went with James and John to the home of Simon and Andrew. Simon's mother-in-law was in bed with a fever, and they immediately told Jesus about her. So he went to her, took her hand and helped her*

up. The fever left her and she began to wait on them. We do not have any information regarding the names of Peter's wife and his mother in Law. Jesus visited them all in Capernaum.

3) **Mark 1: 35-37:** *Very early in the morning, while it was still dark, Jesus got up, left the house and went off to a solitary place, where he prayed. Simon and his companions went to look for him, and when they found him, they exclaimed: "Everyone is looking for you!"* Peter's attitude is very possessive and affirmative in this passage. It will be observable again, later, with the occasion of the "Transfiguration" of Jesus.

4) **Mark 3: 16-17:** *These are the twelve he appointed: Simon (to whom he gave the name Peter), James son of Zebedee and his brother John (to them he gave the name Boanerges, which means "sons of thunder")* This is the fourth time Simon is mentioned in this gospel; this time with the nickname of "stone". The English translation says "Peter".

5) **Mark 5: 21-24 and 35-43:** *When Jesus had again crossed over by boat to the other side of the lake, a large crowd gathered around him while he was by the lake. Then one of the synagogue leaders, named Jairus, came, and when he saw Jesus, he fell at his feet. He pleaded earnestly with him, "My little daughter is dying. Please come and put your hands on her so that she will be healed and live." So, Jesus went with him. ----- While Jesus was still speaking, some people came from the house of Jairus, the synagogue leader. "Your daughter is dead," they said. "Why bother the teacher anymore?" Overhearing what they said, Jesus told him, "Don't be afraid; just believe." He did not let anyone follow him except Peter, James and John the brother of James. When they came to the home of the synagogue leader, Jesus saw a commotion, with people crying and wailing loudly. He went in and said to them, "Why all this commotion and wailing? The child is not dead but asleep." But they laughed at him. After he put them all out, he took the child's father and mother and the disciples who were with him, and went in where the child was. He took her by the hand and said to her, "Talitha koum!" (which means "Little girl, I say to you, get up!").*

Immediately the girl stood up and began to walk around (she was twelve years old). At this they were completely astonished. He gave strict orders not to let anyone know about this, and told them to give her something to eat. Only three apostles were allowed to witness the resurrection of the little girl, a miracle oriented to recommend the power of faith. Peter was one of them. It seems that Jesus wished to fortify Peter's faith on account of his future failure.

6) **Mark 8: 27-30:** *Jesus and his disciples went on to the villages around Caesarea Philippi. On the way he asked them, "Who do people say I am?" They replied, "Some say John the Baptist; others say Elijah; and still others, one of the prophets." "But what about you?" he asked. "Who do you say I am?" Peter answered, "You are the Messiah." Jesus warned them not to tell anyone about him.* In this gospel, we can see Peter's confession without the add-ons which appear in Matthew's gospel. In addition, in chapter nine, we can see that Jesus discovered that the apostles had been discussing whom among them was more important. Jesus took a little boy, placed him among the apostles, and told them that he was more important. In this gospel Jesus' attitude does not show the incongruence seen in Matthew. Here, no apostle is major than the others.

7) **Mark 8: 31-33:** *He then began to teach them that the Son of Man must suffer many things and be rejected by the elders, the chief priests and the teachers of the law, and that he must be killed and after three days rise again. He spoke plainly about this, and Peter took him aside and began to rebuke him. But when Jesus turned and looked at his disciples, he rebuked Peter. "Get behind me, Satan!" he said. "You do not have in mind the concerns of God, but merely human concerns."* Jesus has called Peter "Satan" and used exactly the same words with which He expelled the Devil after the temptation in the Desert. This passage from Mark, confronted with the one from Matthew, cited before, offers a contradiction worthy of detailed study unless we

accept that Matthew 16: 18-19 is a later interpolation and thus all problems are over.

8) **Mark 9: 2-6:** *After six days Jesus took with him Peter and James and John, and led them up a high mountain by themselves. And he was transfigured before them, and his clothes became radiant, intensely white, as no one on earth could bleach them. And there appeared to them Elijah with Moses, and they were talking with Jesus. And Peter said to Jesus, "Rabbi, it is good that we are here. Let us make three tents, one for you and one for Moses and one for Elijah." For he did not know what to say, for they were terrified.* The comment on Peter by the evangelist is very meaningful.

9) **Mark 10: 28:** [28] *Then Peter spoke up, "We have left everything to follow you!".* The thought behind this sentence is obvious: What is our compensation? It is clear that the disciples have been discussing the gains that they will have later in the Kingdom since a few lines later the sons of Zebedee, James and John, ask Jesus to sit down one at His right and the other one at His left later in the Kingdom.

10) **Mark 11: 20-22:** [20] *In the morning, as they went along, they saw the fig tree withered from the roots.* [21] *Peter remembered and said to Jesus, "Rabbi, look! The fig tree you cursed has withered!"* [22] *"Have faith in God," Jesus answered.* [23] *"Truly I tell you, if anyone says to this mountain, 'Go, throw yourself into the sea,' and does not doubt in their heart but believes that what they say will happen, it will be done for them."* Jesus took advantage of the cursed fig tree to teach Peter a tremendous lesson on faith: the power of a firm faith.

11) **Mark 13: 1-13:** *As Jesus was leaving the temple, one of his disciples said to him, "Look, Teacher! What massive stones! What magnificent buildings!" "Do you see all these great buildings?" replied Jesus. "Not one stone here will be left on another; everyone will be thrown down." As Jesus was sitting on the Mount of Olives opposite the temple, Peter, James, John and Andrew asked him privately, "Tell us, when will these things happen? And what will be the sign that they are all about to be fulfilled?" Jesus said to them:*

"Watch out that no one deceives you. Many will come in my name, claiming, 'I am he,' and will deceive many. When you hear of wars and rumors of wars, do not be alarmed. Such things must happen, but the end is still to come. Nation will rise against nation, … (etc.). Notice that Peter is at the same level as James and John. There is no higher category for him or a special distinction.

12) **Mark 14: 27-31:** *"You will all fall away," Jesus told them, for it is written: "I will strike the shepherd, and the sheep will be scattered. But after I have risen, I will go ahead of you into Galilee." Peter declared, "Even if all fall away, I will not." "Truly I tell you," Jesus answered, "today—yes, tonight—before the rooster crows twice, you yourself will disown me three times." But Peter insisted emphatically, "Even if I have to die with you, I will never disown you." And all the others said the same.* Perhaps, we should read these verses in relation to those of Chapter 10 quoted before; Peter did not wish to lose the future gains in the Kingdom.

13) **Mark 14: 32-42:** *They went to a place called Gethsemane, and Jesus said to his disciples, "Sit here while I pray." He took Peter, James and John along with him, and he began to be deeply distressed and troubled. "My soul is overwhelmed with sorrow to the point of death," he said to them. "Stay here and keep watch." Going a little farther, he fell to the ground and prayed that if possible the hour might pass from him. "Abba, Father," he said, "everything is possible for you. Take this cup from me. Yet not what I will, but what you will." Then he returned to his disciples and found them sleeping. "Simon," he said to Peter, "are you asleep? Couldn't you keep watch for one hour? Watch and pray so that you will not fall into temptation. The spirit is willing, but the flesh is weak." Once more he went away and prayed the same thing. When he came back, he again found them sleeping, because their eyes were heavy. They did not know what to say to him. Returning the third time, he said to them, "Are you still sleeping and resting? Enough! The hour has come. Look, the Son of Man is delivered into the hands of sinners. Rise! Let us go! Here comes my betrayer!"* The human side of Jesus suffered a very deep depression worsened by the

fact that his most intimate people did not share his anguish and suffering. After the third unsuccessful visit to the group of his most intimate friends, Jesus gave up. A horde of armed people came and took Jesus to the house of the Supreme Priest.

14) **Mark 14:53-72**: *They took Jesus to the high priest (...) Peter followed him at a distance, right into the courtyard of the high priest. There he sat with the guards and warmed himself at the fire. While Peter was below in the courtyard, one of the servant girls of the high priest came by. When she saw Peter warming himself, she looked closely at him: "You also were with that Nazarene, Jesus," she said. But he denied it. "I don't know or understand what you're talking about," he said, and went out into the entryway. When the servant girl saw him there, she said again to those standing around, "This fellow is one of them." Again, he denied it. After a little while, those standing near said to Peter, "Surely you are one of them, for you are a Galilean." He began to call down curses, and he swore to them, "I don't know this man you're talking about." Immediately the rooster crowed the second time. Then Peter remembered the word Jesus had spoken to him: "Before the rooster crows twice you will disown me three times." And he broke down and wept.* This passage is well-known for its details. Peter's apostasy aggravated by his swearing, and even worse: in front of an insignificant girl. Catastrophic!!! This is the end of Peter's activity in this gospel: "he broke down and wept"!!! What a "primacy"!!!

15) **Mark 16: 1-7**: *When the Sabbath was over, Mary Magdalene, Mary the mother of James, and Salome bought spices so that they might go to anoint Jesus' body. (...) As they entered the tomb, they saw a young man dressed in a white robe sitting on the right side, and they were alarmed. "Don't be alarmed," he said. "You are looking for Jesus the Nazarene, who was crucified. He has risen! (...) go, tell his disciples and Peter, 'He is going ahead of you into Galilee. There you will see him, just as he told you.'"* This is the last cite of Peter in this gospel; he is indirectly mentioned:

"tell the disciples and Peter ..." Probably Peter is specifically mentioned due to his previous apostasy ... but now he is back with the group of disciples. So, he is to be included again. Women become protagonists now; mainly Mary Magdalene mentioned in the first place. The gospel is especially clear and specific: the resurrected Jesus appeared "first" to her. The gospel ends with collective cites of the apostles; they have to go to the whole world and preach to all peoples. There is no mention whatsoever that Peter would possess any primacy or have to supervise his colleagues.

3. The Gospel of Saint Luke

The **Gospel According to Luke** (Greek: Τὸ κατὰ Λουκᾶν εὐαγγέλιον, *to kata Loukan euangelion*) is the third and longest of the four canonical Gospels. It tells of the origins, birth, ministry, death, resurrection and ascension of Jesus Christ.

The most probable date for this gospel is around year 80. The author took for his sources the gospel of Mark, and the collection of sayings called the Q source.

The author assumes an educated Greek-speaking audience, and directs his attention to specifically Christian concerns rather than the Greco-Roman world at large. He begins his gospel with a preface addressed to "Theophilus": the name means "Lover of God," who could be any Christian to whom he encourages faith.

He informs Theophilus of his intention, which is to lead his reader to certainty through an orderly account "of the events that have been fulfilled among us." Regarding the Jews, Luke emphasizes the fact that Jesus and all of his earliest followers were Jews; nevertheless, the Jews had rejected and killed the Messiah, and the Christian mission now lay with the gentiles.[2]

1) **Luke 4:38-43**: *Jesus left the synagogue and went to the home of Simon. Simon's mother-in-law was suffering from a high fever, and*

---

[2] Basic information on the Gospel of Luke has been taken from Wikipedia.

they asked Jesus to help her. So, he bent over her and rebuked the fever, and it left her. She got up at once and began to wait on them. (...)At daybreak, Jesus went out to a solitary place. The people were looking for him and when they came to where he was, they tried to keep him from leaving them. But he said, "I must proclaim the good news of the kingdom of God to the other towns also, because that is why I was sent." This gospel begins with the birth of John the Baptist, goes on with the birth of Jesus and skips to the beginning of his preaching in Judea. Then He goes to Galilee, visits Nazareth, stops at Capernaum and calls on Peter's house where He cures Peter's mother in law who was suffering of a high fever. Then, He declares the main objective of His mission: preaching the Kingdom of God's arrival. He did not come to earth to found churches or start anything but the opposite to announce the end of everything.

2) **Luke 5: 1-11**: *One day as Jesus was standing by the Lake of Gennesaret; the people were crowding around him and listening to the word of God. He saw at the water's edge two boats, (...) He got into one of the boats, the one belonging to Simon, and asked him to put out a little from shore. Then he sat down and taught the people from the boat. When he had finished speaking, he said to Simon, "Put out into deep water, and let down the nets for a catch." Simon answered, "Master, we've worked hard all night and haven't caught anything. But because you say so, I will let down the nets." When they had done so, they caught such a large number of fish that their nets began to break. (...)When Simon Peter saw this, he fell at Jesus' knees and said, "Go away from me, Lord; I am a sinful man!" For he and all his companions were astonished at the catch of fish they had taken, and so were James and John, the sons of Zebedee, Simon's partners. Then Jesus said to Simon, "Don't be afraid; from now on you will fish for people." So, they pulled their boats up on shore, left everything and followed him.* This passage of the miraculous fishing experience offers a depiction of Peter, as a simple and sincere man who becomes aware that the reality of what he is witnessing goes much further than

everyday life. He is also an impulsive and spontaneous man. The promise of "fishing men" was made by Jesus to all the apostles, not only to Peter.

3) **Luke 6: 13-16:** *And when it was day, he called unto him his disciples: and of them he chose twelve, whom also he named apostles; Simon, (whom he also named Peter,) and Andrew his brother, James and John, Philip and Bartholomew, Matthew and Thomas, James the son of Alphaeus, and Simon called Zelotes, And Judas the brother of James, and Judas Iscariot, which also was the traitor.* The election of the first twelve apostles includes only men. Keep in mind that they were to go on solitary roads full of dangers but later Jesus added also many women to His group, and finally Mary Magdalene whom He made the apostle to the apostles as seen in the Gospel of John (John 20:17-and declared so by Pope Saint Hippolyte as early as the third century. The three gospels known as "the synoptic" include this election of the twelve.

4) **Luke 8:43-46:** *And a woman was there who had been subject to bleeding for twelve years but no one could heal her. She came up behind him and touched the edge of his cloak, and immediately her bleeding stopped. "Who touched me?" Jesus asked. When they all denied it, Peter said, "Master, the people are crowding and pressing against you." But Jesus said, "Someone touched me; I know that power has gone out from me."* Obviously, Peter reasons as everybody else, judging by the visible facts.

5) **Luke 8:4-56:** *While Jesus was still speaking, someone came from the house of Jairus, the synagogue leader. "Your daughter is dead," he said. "Don't bother the teacher anymore." Hearing this, Jesus said to Jairus, "Don't be afraid; just believe, and she will be healed." When he arrived at the house of Jairus, he did not let anyone go in with him except Peter, John and James, and the child's father and mother. (...) He took her by the hand and said, "My child, get up!" Her spirit returned, and at once she stood up. Then Jesus told them to give her something to eat. Her parents were astonished, but he*

ordered them not to tell anyone what had happened. Again, the text is focusing on the power of faith: "Do not be afraid, just believe"! Furthermore, Jesus is careful and insists to avoid any sort of exhibitionism.

6) **Luke 9: 18-22:** *Once when Jesus was praying in private and his disciples were with him, he asked them, "Who do the crowds say I am?" They replied, "Some say John the Baptist; others say Elijah; and still others, that one of the prophets of long ago has come back to life." "But what about you?" he asked. "Who do you say I am?" Peter answered, "God's Messiah." Jesus strictly warned them not to tell this to anyone. And he said, "The Son of Man must suffer many things and be rejected by the elders, the chief priests and the teachers of the law, and he must be killed and on the third day be raised to life."* It is obvious that Jesus is answering Peter and definitely forbids him to add anything else on the subject. In addition, He predicts his own death and His immediate resurrection. Nothing else. **Nothing else!** There is no primacy, no keys to Heaven, no tying or untying anything.

Sometime later, a discussion amid the apostles started about who was most important (Luke 9:46). Jesus pointed to a little boy indicating in this way who was to be most important. This discussion on who was to be the most important appears in all four gospels. It is evident then that the gospels do not know anything about any primacy or that Peter was to be the Head of the group.

7) 7) **Luke 9: 28-34:** *About eight days after Jesus said this, he took Peter, John and James with him and went up onto a mountain to pray. As he was praying, the appearance of his face changed, and his clothes became as bright as a flash of lightning. Two men, Moses and Elijah, appeared in glorious splendor, talking with Jesus. They spoke about his departure which he was about to bring to fulfillment at Jerusalem. Peter and his companions were very sleepy, but when they became fully awake, they saw his glory and the two men standing with him. As the men were leaving Jesus,*

Peter said to him, "Master, it is good for us to be here. Let us put up three shelters—one for you, one for Moses and one for Elijah." (He did not know what he was saying.) While he was speaking, a cloud appeared and covered them, and they were afraid as they entered the cloud. This passage narrates the transfiguration of Jesus. Peter says something senseless to the point that even the evangelist enters in the narration to make a comment: "He did not know what he was saying".

8) **Luke 10: 1-20**: *The Lord appointed seventy-two others and sent them two by two ahead of him to every town and place where he was about to go and said: (...) When you enter a house, first say, 'Peace to this house. (...)' and tell them, 'The kingdom of God has come near to you.' But when you enter a town and are not welcomed, go into its streets and say, 'Even the dust of your town we wipe from our feet as a warning to you. Yet be sure of this: The kingdom of God has come near.' I tell you, it will be more bearable on that day for Sodom than for that town. "Woe to you, Chorazin! Woe to you, Bethsaida! For if the miracles that were performed in you had been performed in Tyre and Sidon, they would have repented long ago, sitting in sackcloth and ashes. But it will be more bearable for Tyre and Sidon at the judgment than for you. And you, Capernaum, will you be lifted to the heavens? No, you will go down to Hades. "Whoever listens to you listens to me; whoever rejects you rejects me; but whoever rejects me rejects him who sent me." The seventy-two returned with joy and said, "Lord, even the demons submit to us in your name." He replied, "I saw Satan fall like lightning from heaven. I have given you authority to trample on snakes and scorpions and to overcome all the power of the enemy; nothing will harm you. [20] However, do not rejoice that the spirits submit to you, but rejoice that your names are written in heaven."* Notice that in this passage, the Gospel informs that Jesus had added seventy-two more people to the initial group of twelve. See the powers He confers to them: "**Whoever listens to you, listens to me**". To you all ...! The scribe who interpolated the gospel of Matthew 16:18-19 did not realize that Jesus

gave powers to all and did not come to found churches but on the contrary: to preach that everything ends because the Kingdom of God is coming and for this reason He teaches his disciples to pray to the Father: "May your Kingdom come" (Mat. 6:10).

9) **Luke 12: 41-44**: *Peter asked, "Lord, are you telling this parable to us, or to everyone?" The Lord answered, "Who then is the faithful and wise manager, whom the master puts in charge of his servants to give them their food allowance at the proper time? It will be good for that servant whom the master finds doing so when he returns. Truly I tell you, he will put him in charge of all his possessions.* The parable to which Peter is referring is the one Jesus told in the preceding verses: (Luke 12:32-"Parable of the vigilant servants". Happy are those servants! Probably, Peter was mostly interested in the last part: "the master will put him in charge of all his possessions".

10) **Luke: 22: 7-12**: *Then came the day of Unleavened Bread on which the Passover lamb had to be sacrificed. Jesus sent Peter and John, saying, "Go and make preparations for us to eat the Passover." "Where do you want us to prepare for it?" they asked. He replied, "As you enter the city, a man carrying a jar of water will meet you. Follow him to the house that he enters, and say to the owner of the house, 'The Teacher asks: Where is the guest room, where I may eat the Passover with my disciples?' He will show you a large room upstairs, all furnished. Make preparations there."* Jesus entrusted Peter and John with the preparations required to celebrate Passover, which consisted of a special dinner widely known as the "Last Supper".

11) **Luke 22: 24-30:** *A dispute also arose among them, as to which of them was to be regarded as the greatest (...) He said: let the greatest among you become as the youngest, and the leader as one who serves. For who is the greater, one who reclines at table or one who serves? Is it not the one who reclines at table? But I am among you as the one who serves. "You are those who have stayed with me in my trials, and I assign to you, as my Father assigned*

to me, a kingdom, that you may eat and drink at my table in my kingdom and sit on thrones judging the twelve tribes of Israel. No one is greater than the others; only Jesus is and He gives power equally to all.

12) **Luke 22: 31-34:** *"Simon, Simon, Satan has asked to sift all of you as wheat. But I have prayed for you, Simon, that your faith may not fail. And when you have turned back, strengthen your brothers." But he replied, "Lord, I am ready to go with you to prison and to death." Jesus answered, "I tell you, Peter, before the rooster crows today, you will deny three times that you know me."* This is the famous known text in which Jesus announces Peter 's breakdown. It is attention-grabbing that Jesus first used the word "Simon" but later, referring to the denial, He changed it to Peter (Kefas) which means "little stone".

Nevertheless, Peter will convert later and then he shall fortify the others in order to undo the evil effects of his bad example. Notice that this is not a simple "bad example". Peter clearly committed apostasy upon denying Jesus; he was the first apostate priest in history. This text is followed by the one which narrates Jesus' agony in the Garden of Gethsemane. Jesus asked his apostles to stay awake with Him but they went to sleep. Then, the troop headed by Judas, the traitor, took over the place.

13) **Luke 22:54-62:** *Then seizing him, they led him away and took him into the house of the high priest. Peter followed at a distance. And when some there had kindled a fire in the middle of the courtyard and had sat down together, Peter sat down with them. A servant girl saw him seated there in the firelight. She looked closely at him and said, "This man was with him." But he denied it. "Woman, I don't know him," he said. A little later someone else saw him and said, "You also are one of them." "Man, I am not!", Peter replied. About an hour later another asserted, "Certainly this fellow was with him, for he is a Galilean." Peter replied, "Man, I don't know what you're talking about!" Just as he was speaking, the*

rooster crowed. The Lord turned and looked straight at Peter. Then Peter remembered the word the Lord had spoken to him: "Before the rooster crows today, you will disown me three times." And he went outside and wept bitterly. Peter's denials! They are a true apostasy. All four gospels cite them clearly ascertaining his cowardice, mainly the first one in front of an insignificant girl. In the gospels of Matthew and Mark, the servant girls are two. Upon confirmation, Peter's best reaction was leaving and bitterly crying.

14) **Luke 24: 1-34:** *On the first day of the week, very early in the morning, the women took the spices they had prepared and went to the tomb. (...) They did not find the body of the Lord Jesus. (...) Two men in clothes that gleamed like lightning stood beside them. (...)The men said to them, (...) He is not here; he has risen! (...) They told all these things to the Eleven and to all the others. (...) But they did not believe the women, because their words seemed to them like nonsense. Peter, however, got up and ran to the tomb. Bending over, he saw the strips of linen lying by themselves, and he went away, wondering to himself what had happened. Now that same day two of them were going to a village called Emmaus, about seven miles from Jerusalem. They were talking with each other about everything that had happened. As they talked and discussed these things, Jesus himself came up and walked along with them; but they were kept from recognizing him. He asked them, "What are you discussing together as you walk along?" They stood still, their faces downcast. One of them, named Cleopas, asked him, "Are you the only one visiting Jerusalem who does not know the things that have happened there in these days?" "What things?" he asked. "About Jesus of Nazareth," they replied. (...) Some of our women amazed us. They went to the tomb early this morning but didn't find his body. They came and told us that they had seen a vision of angels, who said he was alive. (...) They got up and returned at once to Jerusalem. There they found the Eleven and those with them, assembled together and saying, "It is true! The Lord has risen and has appeared to Simon."* This text is highly

complicated and contradictory. In the Gospel of Matthew, Jesus appeared first to two women, Mary Magdalena and the other Mary. In the Gospel of Mark, Jesus first appeared to Mary Magdalene. In the Gospel of John, Jesus appeared first and very especially to Mary Magdalene with an exchange of conversation. In this Gospel of Luke, two men dressed with brilliant clothing are the ones who tell the women that Jesus has resurrected, and the women inform the apostles. Peter goes to see but only finds abandoned shrouds and returns without seeing anybody amazed at what had happened. The text clearly states that one of them (Peter) went to investigate and found true what women had said: there was no body but he did not see anybody. In this Gospel of Luke, Jesus does not appear to anybody but to two men traveling to Emmaus. Then, these men tell the apostles that Jesus had appeared to Peter. The contradictions **are not** from one Gospel to another but within the very text of this one. And this is the last time Peter is mentioned individually although collectively it is supposed that he was present at the ascension of the Lord into Heaven.

4. <u>The Gospel of Saint John</u>

The Gospel According to John, in Greek: Τὸ κατὰ Ἰωάννην εὐαγγέλιον, *to kata Ioannen euangelion*) is the fourth canonical gospel in the New Testament, after the synoptic gospels of Matthew, Mark, and Luke.

John begins with the witness and affirmation of John the Baptist and concludes with the death, burial, resurrection, and post-resurrection appearances of Jesus. This gospel considerably differs from the previous ones not only because of its literary style but also for its content. It was written in Greek by an anonymous author. It identifies its author as "the disciple whom Jesus loved." Although the text does not name this disciple, by the beginning of the 2nd century, a tradition had begun to form which identified him with John the Apostle, one of the Twelve (Jesus' innermost circle). Although some notable New Testament scholars affirm traditional Johannine scholarship, the majority do not believe that John or any one of the Apostles wrote it and attribute it instead to a "Johannine community" which traced its traditions to John; the gospel itself shows signs of having been composed in three "layers", reaching its final form about 90–100 AD.

The Scholar Bart Ehrman argues that there are differences in the composition of the Greek within the Gospel, such as breaks and inconsistencies in sequence, repetitions in the discourse, as well as passages that he believes do not belong to their context, and suggest redaction.

Conservative scholars consider internal evidences, such as not mentioning the destruction of the Temple and a number of passages that they consider characteristics of an eyewitness, sufficient evidence that the gospel was composed around the year 100.

1) **John 1: 40-42:** *Andrew, Simon Peter's brother, was one of the two who heard what John had said and who had followed Jesus. The first thing Andrew did was to find his brother Simon and tell him, "We have found the Messiah" (that is, the Christ). And he brought him to Jesus. Jesus looked at him and said, "You are Simon son of John. You will be called Cephas" (which, when translated, is Peter).* This is the first time the exact word used by Jesus to call Peter --Cephas in Aramaic-- appears in the gospels. The Greek version is πετρος (Petros = stone). The English language gives "Peter".

2) **John 6:8:** *One of his disciples, Andrew, Simon Peter's brother, said unto him: There is a lad here, which hath five barley loaves, and two small fishes: but what are they among so many?* Simon continues to be called "Simon-Stone", although the English translation gives it as "Simon Peter".

3) **John 6:66-69:** *From this time many of his disciples turned back and no longer followed him. "You do not want to leave too, do you?" Jesus asked the Twelve. Simon Peter answered him, "Lord, to whom*

shall we go? You have the words of eternal life. We have come to believe and to know that you are the Holy One of God." Simon-Stone is always ready. In this case, the Gospel of John declares that many left Jesus when He told them that His flesh was true food and his blood, true drink and that whoever ate it will live eternally.

4) **John 13: 1-9:** *It was just before the Passover Festival. (... After that, he poured water into a basin and began to wash his disciples' feet, drying them with the towel that was wrapped around him. He came to Simon Peter, who said to him, "Lord, are you going to wash my feet?" Jesus replied, "You do not realize now what I am doing, but later you will understand. "No," said Peter, "you shall never wash my feet." Jesus answered, "Unless I wash you, you have no part with me. "Then, Lord," Simon Peter replied, "not just my feet but my hands and my head as well!"* Peter's answer **always** reveals the same, a simple and impulsive man.

5) **John 13: 21-28:** *After he had said this, Jesus was troubled in spirit and testified, "Very truly I tell you, one of you is going to betray me." His disciples stared at one another, at a loss to know which of them he meant. One of them, the disciple whom Jesus loved, was reclining next to him. Simon Peter motioned to this disciple and said, "Ask him which one he means." Leaning back against Jesus, he asked him, "Lord, who is it?" Jesus answered, "It is the one to whom I will give this piece of bread when I have dipped it in the dish." Then, dipping the piece of bread, he gave it to Judas, the son of Simon Iscariot. As soon as Judas took the bread, Satan entered into him. So, Jesus told him, "What you are about to do, do quickly." But no one at the meal understood* why Jesus said this to him. Peter appears in this text much more distant and strange to Jesus to the point that he is requesting a favor from a companion in order to address the Lord. At the end of the last supper, Jesus announced to his disciples that the time He still had with them, would be very short and that the place He was going they could not go.

6) **John 13: 36-38:** *Simon Peter asked him, "Lord, where are you going?" Jesus replied, "Where I am going, you cannot follow now, but you will follow later." Peter asked, "Lord, why can't I follow you now? I will lay down my life for you." Then Jesus answered, "Will you really lay down your life for me? Very truly I tell you, before the rooster crows, you will disown me three times!* Peter appears here as the same very impulsive man. Jesus calls him to his true reality pre-announcing his future denials. After a few interventions by other apostles, as Thomas and Philip, Jesus pronounces His supreme speech, promises the coming of the Holy Spirit, and gives them His peace. He makes the comparison of the vine shoots, and declares the depth of His love for them and the future disciples. Finally, He prophesizes persecutions against them on account of His name, and ends with His prayer to the Father.

7) **John 18: 1-11:** *When he had finished praying, Jesus left with his disciples and crossed the Kidron Valley. On the other side there was a garden, and he and his disciples went into it. Now Judas, who betrayed him, knew the place, (...)and came to the garden, guiding a detachment of soldiers and some officials from the chief priests and the Pharisees. (...) Jesus, knowing all that was going to happen to him, went out and asked them, "Who is it you want?" "Jesus of Nazareth," they replied. "I am he," Jesus said. (...). If you are looking for me, then let these men go." This happened so that the words he had spoken would be fulfilled: "I have not lost one of those you gave me. Then Simon Peter, who had a sword, drew it and struck the high priest's servant, cutting off his right ear. (The servant's name was Malchus.) Jesus commanded Peter, "Put your sword away! Shall I not drink the cup the Father has given me?"* Jesus commanded Peter to put away the sword because no one should obstruct His Father's will. Jesus was imprisoned and taken to the house of Annas and later to Caiaphas, the High Priest.

8) **John 18: 15-27:** *Simon Peter and another disciple were following Jesus. Because this disciple was known to the high priest, he went*

with Jesus into the high priest's courtyard (...) Then the servant girl told Peter "You aren't one of this man's disciples too, are you?" she asked Peter. He replied, "I am not." It was cold, and the servants and officials stood around a fire they had made to keep warm. Peter also was standing with them, warming himself. Meanwhile, the high priest questioned Jesus about his disciples and his teaching....) Then Annas sent him bound to Caiaphas the high priest. Meanwhile, Simon Peter was still standing there warming himself. So they asked him, "You aren't one of his disciples too, are you?" He denied it, saying, "I am not." One of the high priest's servants, a relative of the man whose ear Peter had cut off, challenged him, "Didn't I see you with him in the garden?" Again, Peter denied it, and at that moment a rooster began to crow. Peter's denials are accurately narrated in all four gospels; nevertheless, in this one the details are total. Peter's apostasy is extremely obvious and shameful in front of an insignificant servant.

9) **John 20: 1-23:** *Early on the first day of the week, while it was still dark, Mary Magdalene went to the tomb and saw that the stone had been removed from the entrance. So, she came running to Simon Peter and the other disciple, the one Jesus loved, and said, "They have taken the Lord out of the tomb, and we don't know where they have put him!" So, Peter and the other disciple started for the tomb. Both were running, but the other disciple outran Peter and reached the tomb first. He bent over and looked in at the strips of linen lying there but did not go in. Then Simon Peter came along behind him and went straight into the tomb. He saw the strips of linen lying there, (...). Finally, the other disciple, who had reached the tomb first, also went inside. He saw and believed. (...) Mary Magdalene went to the disciples with the news: "I have seen the Lord!" And she told them that he had said these things to her. On the evening of that first day of the week, when the disciples were together, with the doors locked for fear of the Jewish leaders, Jesus came and stood among them and said, "Peace be with you!" After he said this, he showed them his hands and side. The disciples were overjoyed when they saw the Lord. Again, Jesus said, "Peace*

be with you! As the Father has sent me, I am sending you." And with that he breathed on them and said, *"Receive the Holy Spirit. If you forgive anyone's sins, their sins are forgiven; if you do not forgive them, they are not forgiven."* Mary Magdalene was facing a case of criminal justice --the theft of a corpse, and for this reason she went to Peter whom she knew armed and brave. The resurrected Jesus appeared to her first and then to the disciples. That Mary Magdalene entered the tomb and that she was to touch the dead body and that the resurrected Jesus appeared first to her shows that she was His wife because, according to the laws, no one else was allowed to do all of that.

Later, Jesus commissions the disciples and gives them all the power to forgive or not forgive sins, to all of them, not to Peter alone. In the Gospel of Luke (10:16) Jesus adds: *"The one who hears you hears me, and the one who rejects you rejects me, and the one who rejects me rejects him who sent me."* All the apostles and disciples received the same powers. There is no one who has received more and there is not any primacy.

10) **John 21: 1-14:** 21 *Afterward Jesus appeared again to his disciples, by the Sea of Galilee. It happened this way: Simon Peter, Thomas (also known as Didymus), Nathanael from Cana in Galilee, the sons of Zebedee, and two other disciples were together. "I'm going out to fish," Simon Peter told them, and they said, "We'll go with you." So, they went out and got into the boat, but that night they caught nothing. Early in the morning, Jesus stood on the shore, but the disciples did not realize that it was Jesus. He called out to them, "Friends, haven't you any fish?" "No", they answered. He said, "Throw your net on the right side of the boat and you will find some." When they did, they were unable to haul the net in because of the large number of fish. Then the disciple whom Jesus loved said to Peter, "It is the Lord!" As soon as Simon Peter heard him say, "It is the Lord," he wrapped his outer garment around him*

(for he was naked) and jumped into the water. The other disciples followed in the boat, towing the net full of fish, for they were not far from shore, about a hundred yards. (...) This was the third time Jesus appeared to his disciples after he was raised from the dead. After the resurrection of Jesus, Peter did not engage in any apostolic activity, suitable for one holding a primacy; he simply went back to his old capacity, fishing, naked. This is all he could think about after Jesus' resurrection.

11) **John 21: 15-17:** *When they had finished eating, Jesus said to Simon Peter, "Simon son of John, do you love me more than these?" "Yes, Lord", he said, "you know that I love you." Jesus said, "Feed my lambs. Again, Jesus said, "Simon son of John, do you love "me?" He answered, "Yes, Lord, you know that I love you", Peter said, "Take care of my sheep." The third time he said to him, "Simon son of John, do you love me?" Peter was hurt because Jesus asked him the third time, "Do you love me?" He said, "Lord, you know all things; you know that I love you." Jesus said, "Feed my sheep.* Much foolishness has been written about this text, even to the assertion that it is the best exponent of Peter's primacy. (???)

Let's first study the word "love". The English translation, "love", does not exactly reflect the original Greek text which uses two different words for it: "agapein" and "philein". Both are generally translated as "to love"; nevertheless, "love" = **"agape"** is a love based on admiration and respect; it is a love of a lasting character; it implies sacrifice and is totally disinterested and giving, ready to serve. It is the word in *"For God so **loved** the world that He gave his only begotten Son".* (John 3:16). This is precisely the verb which Jesus used in His question: *"Simon, son of John, do you love me? ("Simon Ioannou, **agapás** me ...?)* The other word for love is "philein"; it is a love based on affection; it is a rather impulsive love, susceptible to easily cooling down. This is the verb used by Peter in all his answers: *"Yes, Lord, you know that I **love** you"* (oti **philo** te). Peter did not dare to answer the Lord's question by affirming a love capable of the most accomplished sacrifices since he had just finished his triple denial of Jesus during the Lord's most tragic moments. This is the reason for the word love/philein instead of the word used by Jesus, love/agapein. Jesus repeated the question and Peter answered in the same way, using the word "philein". Jesus did not accept hasty and superficial answers. Peter had to appeal to his deepest feelings when Jesus confronted him. Finally, Jesus descended to Peter's level and in the third question used Peter's word "philein" as if He doubted Peter's unconditional love. It is not strange that Peter became sad and appealed to Jesus' omniscient comprehension.

The next step is analyzing Jesus' demand: 1) "Feed my lambs", 2) "take care of my sheep" and 3) "Feed my sheep". The ill-advised explanations which have been written about this section have gone to the point of altering the sequence of this text in order to produce a non-existent gradation. The correct Greek phrases are: a) "boske ta arnia = "feed my lambs"; b) "poimaine ta probata" = "take care of my sheep" and c) "boske ta probata" = "feed my sheep". Now, consider that Peter had gone astray with his denials of Jesus; this is to say that upon denying Jesus, Peter had abandoned his apostolic mission of taking care of Jesus' flock. He was an apostate, a traitor; he was the first apostate priest in history, a renegade: he had given up his apostolic mission. Now, in his infinite mercy, Jesus entrusted him again with his apostolic mission of feeding and taking care of the flock, both the lambs (a word which appears only once) and the sheep (a word which appears twice -- the second and the third mention), which he had disowned.[3]

Peter had committed perjury on top of abandoning his apostolic mission. Now, Jesus accepted him back. Nothing of Roman imperialistic dreams! In addition, notice the triple repetition in Jesus' declaration; it parallels Peter's previous triple negation.

12) **John 21: 18-23:** *Very truly I tell you, when you were younger you dressed yourself and went where you wanted; but when you are*

---

[3] On this text, a very foolish collection of nonsense has been written; I have just seen an explanation solemnly declaring that the text signifies the confirmation of PETER'S primacy in Rome (¿¿¿????).

old you will stretch out your hands, and someone else will dress you and lead you where you do not want to go." Jesus said this to indicate the kind of death by which Peter would glorify God. Then he said to him, "Follow me!" Peter turned and saw that the disciple whom Jesus loved was following them. (This was the one who had leaned back against Jesus at the supper and had said, "Lord, who is going to betray you?") When Peter saw him, he asked, "Lord, what about him?" Jesus answered, "If I want him to remain alive until I return, what is that to you? You must follow me." Because of this, the rumor spread among the believers that this disciple would not die. But Jesus did not say that he would not die; he only said, "If I want him to remain alive until I return, what is that to you?" Many scholars consider this final paragraph a later addition. This section seems to come to the issue whether after the death of the main first representatives of Christianity (Jacob, Jesus' brother, year 62 and Simon Peter about year 64), John was supposed to survive until Christ's second coming.[4]

Commentary on the preceding gospels

Up to this point, all texts referring to Peter, Simon, Simon Peter, or Kephas, in the canonical gospels have been transcribed. The sum of passages in which he appears is as follows: fourteen times in Matthew, fifteen in Mark, fourteen in Luke, and twelve in John. A total of fifty-five passages. Now, in reference to the words themselves (being they Simon, Peter, Simon Peter, or Kephas) the numbers are the following: twenty five in Matthew, twenty five in Mark, thirty in Luke, and forty in John. A total of 120 mentions.

As seen in these texts, with the exception of Matthew 16:18 (that

---

[4] Thus, this chapter may have been written in about year sixty-five on without the possibility of being more precise. Chapter twenty ends with the section that would be the real epilogue of this gospel: John 20: 30-31, which would be the conclusion of the whole gospel. Nevertheless, Chapter 21 continues with the narrations about the resurrected Jesus as if the epilogue was nonexistent. At the end of Chapter 21, a new conclusion is given: John 21: 24-25.

we shall study later) no primacy of Peter exists, or keys, or binding or unbinding of any sort that has not been given equally to all as seen in John 20:21: *Again, Jesus said, "Peace be with you! As the Father has sent me, I am sending you." And with that he breathed on them and said, "Receive the Holy Spirit. If you forgive anyone's sins, their sins are forgiven; if you do not forgive them, they are not forgiven."*

Here, we find a mention of powers --forgive, or do not forgive-- but those powers are equally given to all of the disciples. In addition, given the animosity that Peter developed against women, especially against Mary Magdalene, it is necessary to make a careful study of such hostility since it became the origin of the official exclusion of women from the church leadership and ministry positions, particularly in the Church of Rome up to our days. Consequently, this work contains a second part dedicated to Mary Magdalene.

The inconsistent and anomalous character of Peter is not only observable in the recently discovered Gnostic gospels (that we shall study later) where he wishes that women be expelled from the group of the disciples but also in the Canonical gospels where he appears demanding from Jesus to be able to walk on the water as a condition to believe in Him (Math. 14:28). Later he disowned Jesus in front of everybody when the situation became tense (Math. 26:70). In Gethsemane, he carried a weapon and harmed a servant of the High Priest (John 18:10). Nevertheless, he was afraid of an insignificant girl and, when things became critical, he went to sleep (Mark 14:37) to finally disappear completely in the most critical moments of Jesus' life.

The election of Peter attributed to Jesus *"You are Peter and on this rock I will build my church"* appears only in the chapter 16, verses 18 and 19 of the Gospel of Matthew, and is totally <u>unacceptable</u>. No other section in this same gospel refers to it or seems to know of it. No other gospel quotes it despite the importance that it should have. All the important facts in the life of Jesus are mentioned in all gospels, such as His baptism and Saint John the Baptist, Jesus' initiation into public life, the agony in Gethsemane, the crucifixion, etc.

By the way, the word "kephas" that supposedly Jesus used in

this text, which appears in the Gospel of Matthew, does not mean "rock" or "fundamental cornerstone" at all. In Aramaic, Arabian, or other Semitic languages, "kephas" is a small green stone, used for the purpose of divination. In the text of the Matthew gospel quoted above, Jesus used the word as a nickname for one of His disciples, Simon, who had just guessed that Jesus was the Christ (thanks to the Celestial Father's inspiration.) The **Roman** Bible commentators translate the word "kephas" as a "stone", and conclude that Peter was the fundamental corner stone of the Church, symbolized as a building, a conclusion entirely <u>unacceptable</u> because fundamental stone in Hebrew is "Pin-nah" and not "kephas". In the Scriptures, Jesus is the "pin-nah" of Christianity because it compares the Church of the building previously prophesized by Isaias (28:16); a building to which God Himself would give a fundamental rock. Saint Paul interprets it very appropriately when in his letter to the Ephesians (2:20-21) tells us: ²⁰ **built on the foundation of the apostles and prophets, <u>with Christ Jesus himself as the chief cornerstone</u>.⁵ In him the whole building is joined together and rises to become a holy temple in the Lord.**

The apostle Peter also quoted the rock and referred it to Jesus Christ: *⁴As you come to him, the living Stone—rejected by humans but chosen by God and precious to him— ⁵you also, like living stones, are being built into a spiritual house[a] to be a holy priesthood, offering spiritual sacrifices acceptable to God through Jesus Christ. ⁶For in Scripture it says:*

> *"See, I lay a stone in Zion,*
> *a chosen and precious **cornerstone**,*
> *and the one who trusts in him*
> *will never be put to shame."* (I Peter: 2: 4-6)

Psalm 118:2 reveals that "the *stone rejected by the builders has become the cornerstone*". In Hebrew "rosch pin-nah. Jesus quoted it and applied it to Himself. See the very same Gospel of Matthew

---

⁵ (In Paul's original word, in Greek, it is "akrogoniaiou", which literally means: "akro" = "end, tip" plus "gonía" = "projecting corner" = "corner foundation stone")

21:42-44: Jesus said to them, "Have you never read in the Scriptures: "The stone the builders rejected has become the cornerstone; the Lord has done this, and it is marvelous in our eyes? Therefore, I tell you that the kingdom of God will be taken away from you and given to a people who will produce its fruit. Anyone who falls on this stone will be broken to pieces; anyone on whom it falls will be crushed."

See as well Mark 12:10-11 and Luke 20:17. Peter took this prophecy for his third speech, the one given to the whole meeting of the Sanhedrim as quoted in the book Acts of the Apostles (4: 12) : *"He is the stone rejected by you, builders, which has become the cornerstone and there is no salvation in anyone else."*

In addition, Matthew's gospel is taken from the previous Mark's gospel, which in the corresponding passage says nothing about any foundation of the church or about Peter as the fundamental rock which, by the way, is **blasphemous** since it takes away Jesus' main function as the church angular stone, as it was preannounced by the prophets, in order to give it to a human being.

Furthermore, it seems absolutely incongruent giving Peter such an importance in chapter sixteen to conclude shortly after with a poor and insignificant statement: *"He went outside and cried bitterly"* (Math. 26:75), and this is the last time Peter is mentioned in this gospel, the "Primacy" gospel (???).

The Roman Catholic Church takes this "Matthew 16" text as the foundation of its alleged supremacy above all other Christian churches; nevertheless, being of such a magnitude, this text should appear in all other gospels and books of the New Testament, and in all early Roman writers, as it is obvious, to give fundament to its power. At the same time, if this text had originally existed, all the Apostolic Fathers [6] should have mentioned it, mainly when they referred to the Church of Rome -as St. Ignatius (35-107), bishop of Antioch in his letter to the Romans: *"to the one which presides in the region of the Romans"*. There, only in that place!

Didache or *The Teaching of the Twelve Apostles* was an important

---

[6] They are the witnesses of the early stages of Christianity (centuries one and two).

document, probably the first known work of Christian literature, written during the second half of the first century. Not even indirectly does it presuppose Peter's primacy or Rome as head of Christianity.

Saint Polycarp, bishop of Smyrna, in what is today Turkey was another apostolic father. He was decided on establishing the date of Easter and consulted all bishops, including Rome. He was not able to find a solution because Polycarp appealed to the authority of Saint John and the apostles while Anicetus, bishop of Rome, preferred to follow the traditions of his predecessors. Again, nothing about any primacy or Peter in Rome.

The Shepherd of Hermas was a highly appreciated book in the early church to the point that several Fathers of the Church considered it part of the Sacred Scripture. The book reflects on the early conditions of Roman Christianity in the middle of the Second Century. Always, the same: not even a minuscule mention of Peter, rock, or primacy of any sort.

Papias, bishop of Hierapolis in Frygia, Asia Minor (today Turkey) who, according to St. Irenaeus, was a disciple of the apostle John and a friend of Polycarp, wrote around year 130 five books on *Explanations of the Lord's Sayings*, which the scholars consider the first work of exegesis on the gospels. Nothing about Peter's primacy or Rome.

Saint Justine, martyr (100-165), who lived, wrote and died in Rome during the early years of the Second Century never mentioned that Peter might have been there and even less that he had founded the Church of Rome.

It is not intended to be repetitive but it is obvious that Peter's primacy and the famous *"You are Peter and on this rock, I will build my church"* was totally unknown to the early Christians.

Probably, this passage in the Gospel of Matthew has been inserted around the first years of the fourth century, perhaps under the Papacy of Julius I and his attempts to establish the supremacy of the Roman Church, as we shall see later. The text appears in the oldest copies of the New Testament that we possess: Codex Sinaiticus and Codex Vaticanus, both from the middle of the fourth century.

In addition, this text is completely foreign to the scope and intentions of Jesus. Nowhere in the New Testament is said that Jesus came to earth to build a church, or an institution, or start anything of the sort. On the contrary, His preaching was eschatological, the end of all things is coming, the Kingdom of God is at the doors. Jesus spent his days on earth proclaiming the good news of the Kingdom, the Kingdom of God, which soon was to be established on earth and the wicked would be thrown out, as per Mathew 4:23: "*He went round the whole of Galilee (...) proclaiming the good news of the Kingdom*" and Mark 1:15: "*The time is fulfilled and the Kingdom of God is close at hand*".

Furthermore, Peter himself in his letters, as Paul in his own, never ever mentions a foundation stone on Peter or anybody else. On the contrary, both of them declare that the one and only foundation stone is Jesus Christ. See the first letter of Paul to the Corinthians, chapter three, verse eleven: "*For nobody can lay down any other foundation than the one which is there already, namely Jesus Christ*":

ακρογωνιαιos = akrogoniaios = **corner foundation stone** as we have seen it before in the letter to the Ephesians (See footnote number eight).

Regarding Peter, read his first letter, chapter two, verses four through eight, where referring to Jesus, he says:

> *He* (Jesus Christ) *is the living stone, rejected by human beings but chosen by God and precious to Him*". (...) *As Scripture says: "Now I am laying a stone in Zion, a chosen, precious cornerstone and no one who relies on this will be brought to disgrace". To you, believers, it brings honor; but for unbelievers, it is rather a stone which the builders rejected that became a cornerstone, a stumbling stone, a rock to trip people up. They stumble over it because they do not believe in the Word.*

This is more than obvious; Jesus Christ is the one and only foundation stone of the Church. There is no other rock on which

His church may be built. The text interpolated in the Gospel of Matthew --Peter is the foundational rock-- is not only against the Scriptures but it is also blasphemous for appropriating to a human a divine attribute.

Even more: that text is incompatible with the context; a few lines down, Jesus calls Peter "Satan" (verse 23): *"Get behind me, Satan! You are an obstacle in my path because you are thinking not as God thinks but as human beings do".*

Notice as well that the alleged Peter's preeminence does not coincide with other evangelical texts in which Jesus manifests his position. See as an example the passage in the Gospel of John chapter twenty, in which Jesus after His resurrection waits until Peter leaves the place in order to appear to Mary Magdalene and ask her to inform Peter and all the disciples of His decisions. It is not possible to assume that Jesus did it inadvertently as neither is it possible that Peter did not realize that he was being postponed to a woman; and, perhaps, this was the cause of the impolite treatment he gave Mary and the other women when they informed him about the empty tomb. (Luke 24:11). He really treated them as insane. In the *Gospel of Mary*, Peters says that "Mary must leave because women are not worthy of life".

Additionally, the New Testament book, <u>Acts of the Apostles</u>, which will be immediately studied, never indicates that Peter could have been a fundamental stone of any church. Much on the contrary, it solemnly declares that Jesus Christ is the only foundation on which salvation for the human kind is firmly established (Acts 4:11-12). More than this, in this very same book of the New Testament, we learn that the just born Christian Church was governed by the collective conduction of the apostles. See chapters 4:36 and 6:2-7 as sufficient examples. See also Acts 15:22: *"The apostles and the presbyters with whole church decided ...*

The twelve apostles not only mandated the call of all the disciples but they also specifically ordered Peter to go and preach in Samaria (Acts 8:14). Moreover, when they realized that the growth of the Church was more and more noticeable, they decided to create a new post at the administrative top of the church, the diaconate, and ordained the first deacons for the church service (Acts 6:1-7). Finally, when the convocation of a Church assembly was deemed necessary (the first Ecumenical Council) Peter was not the one who called for it and then presided over it but Jacob, Jesus' brother (Acts, Chapter 15). Jacob, then, summarized the issues which had been discussed, drew up the conclusions and proclaimed them. Then, the apostles and the presbyters approved them.

Moreover, the fact that Peter moved to and lived in Rome, and was its first bishop is entirely impossible. Peter's presence in Rome cannot be honestly upheld. Someone would have mentioned him. Saint Paul in his letter to the Romans in the year 57 would have greeted him as he acknowledged everybody even the most unknown. How could it be possible that he had omitted his salutation for the "Prince of Apostles"? As a matter of fact, when St. Paul traveled through Antioch, he mentioned Peter (although to rebuke him), who was there but on Peter in Rome there is absolutely nothing! All we have about Peter in Rome are late legends. We shall study later the great need for the Church of Rome to get an apostle "founder" in order to compete with the Christian earlier towns. Many scholars believe that Peter must have died in Antioch, the most faraway known place he visited. Nevertheless, the ossuary recently found in a Christian cemetery in the Mount of Olives, near Jerusalem, with his name written in Aramaic, his native tongue, "Shimon bar Jona" = Simon, son of John, (Math. 16:17) makes it possible to believe that he never left his place of origin and that there he died.

Despite the efforts of Pope Pius XII to demonstrate that he had found Saint Peter's tomb in the Vatican, it is absolutely certain that he did not find it. The earliest church of Saint Peter was built during the Fourth Century as a small temple on a property which had been a pagan cemetery. If Peter had traveled to Rome, had established a Christian community there, and had been its bishop, obviously he would not have been buried in a pagan cemetery and his mortal remains simply thrown anywhere. Certainly, Pius XII may have found first century human remains there -- that place having been a cemetery-- but he was not able to produce any type of identification of such remains.

Evidently, if Peter had been the bishop of Rome, his burial

place should had been distinguished with some kind of honorific decorations and inscriptions, at least his name written on the ossuary as the one found on the Mont of Olives and someone, some writer, should have mentioned it ... but nothing! Despite this absence of proof, the successor of Pope Pius, Paul VI ordered the construction of a magnificent staircase in the center of the Vatican basilica leading to a rich crystal urn which contains another one, made of pure gold, with a title "St. Peter's tomb". An official lie but how efficient considering the millions of pilgrims who visit the place!

Besides, Peter could not have ever been the "bishop" of Rome for the simple reason that, in those days, bishops did not exist yet. The first Christian communities were born in family houses, even administered by women, as we can see, without any room for doubts, in the letter of Saint Paul to the Romans. When those early Christian communities grew, they were led by the institution of elders --presbyteroi-- sort of administrators[7] who were not yet absolute chiefs or monarchs over a church, as it happened by the end of the Second Century on.

The first Christian groups which appeared in Rome in those days were rather small and they gathered in family houses as we have seen before, and they were even administered by women (the house wives) who were in charge of the Eucharistic meal as can be seen in the New Testament, in the already mentioned Paul's letter to the Romans, and in neighborhoods of Greek immigrants (Saint Paul wrote to them in Greek). They did not feel Romans yet nor intimately realized that Rome was the head of the world but soon they would become conscious of that and they would feel the need for a great founder, an apostle, an evangelist, as the other Christian centers which had become famous in those days, such as Antioch, Ephesus, or Alexandria which proudly showed off illustrious creators, such as John, Paul, Philip, or Mark ... but in Rome, the head of the world ... Nothing!!! They were too far from the cradle of Christianity, did not have sanctuaries or sacred tombs,

---

[7] The Greek word "presbyteros" means "older". The English word "bishop" comes from Greek "Episkopos" which means the "one who looks from above", the "supervisor" in Latin.

or great theologians but they were the center of the world and it was urgent to have and exhibit their own apostle and why only one and not two like Peter and Paul for example?[8]

For this, it was necessary to have a biblical text which would make Peter someone important among the apostles, not just a coward who disowned Jesus in His most tragic moments. It would be very convenient to account for with a biblical text which would declare something like: *"You are Peter and on this rock I will build my church"*, for example, and --of course-- it was necessary to bring him to Rome. To Rome!!! Why Rome and not Jerusalem? The early Christians did not have anything to do with Rome and even less, Jesus.

The most surprising is **how** this gospel of Matthew finishes its mentions of Peter. The last reference to Peter is: *"and he went outside and wept bitterly"* after his denial of Jesus (Matthew 26: 75). After this mention, he disappears. Amazing conclusion for one holding a primacy!

It is obvious that whoever interpolated the famous text *You are Peter and super hanc petram...* etc. did not realize that he should have added something else, something more in accord with the primacy to make sense. Most probably it would be impossible now a days to know who inserted this famous text into Matthew's gospel but, at least, we may affirm that they were Romans who spoke Latin; the play of words *"Petrus/petra"* (Peter/petra) only works in Latin, or Greek; it does not have any meaning in Aramaic, Jesus' language. Jesus could not have said it. At the same time, the fact that Peter appears as the head of this Roman church is an evident result of the struggle for power that we will further discuss later.

In addition, the Graeco-Roman concept of "ecclesia" (church) [9] could not have meant anything to Jesus in whose experience only existed

---

[8] Despite that Saint Paul addressed his letter to the Romans, people who were Christians before his arrival.

[9] So, I now say to you: you are Peter and on this rock, I will build my church (ecclesiam), (Matthew16: 18). In Latin: "Et ego dico tibi, quia tu es Petrus et super hanc petram edificabo ecclesiam meam". In Greek: "Kagw de soi legw oti su ei petros, kai epi tauth th petra oikodomhsw mou thn ekklhsian.

the "synagogue" whose reality was and still is completely different. The term "ecclesia" appears in the text of Matthew quoted above as an item known by everybody: "I will build my church (ecclesia)" **but it was not!!!** Nor Jesus or His poor disciples, fishermen of Galilee, may have known the word "εκκλησια" = "ecclesia" = church, which was a Greek pagan and aristocratic organization; it was an assembly of citizens of Athens, older than eighteen years of age, born in Athens and sons of Athenian citizens as well, who gathered forty times a year on the Pnyx hill in the center of Athens to honor their god. In the daily life of the Jews, both elements, the word and its meaning, were totally nonexistent. Jesus could not know it or say it, or his disciples understand it, or Matthew write it. It is more than evident that this word reveals a later experience, posterior to the moment that is attributed in the Matthew gospel. This word never appears in the Jewish Bible or in the gospels, except in Matthew 18:17 ("if someone does not obey, tell the church") which also must be an interpolation because such an organization did not exist among the Jews. Only later, when the Christians began to have contacts with the Greek world, the word "ecclesia" appeared in the New Testament books although with a different meaning.[10]

We should also remember that, when Saul (Paul) was accepted into the Christian community after his conversion he was greeted in Jerusalem by three leaders whom he called "columns" or "pillars" (Gal.2:9); the first one was Jacob, Jesus' brother, and the others Peter and John. They sent him to preach to the pagans; Peter and John would do it for the Jews. The center of Christianity was Jerusalem.

Additionally, that Peter would become the apostle of pagan Rome contradicted the agreement celebrated in Jerusalem, confirmed by leaders of the first Christian church: Paul to the pagans and Peter to the Jews. It is not necessary to remark that this agreement could not have been be established in any other way: Paul was Greek and his

---

[10] In the Acts of the Apostles the word appears twenty times; in St. Paul, who traveled throughout the Greek world, sixty two times; in St,. James, only one ; In Peter's letters, amazingly none; In John's letters, three times; in Jude, none; in the Apocalypse, 15 times, in reference to the churches of Asia Minor (today Turkey).

native tongue was Greek. Peter, a Jew, did not speak any other language but Aramaic; he was a poor fisherman, illiterate and ignorant. What language could he speak in Rome? The agreement was fulfilled by them as we can see in their letters, those of Paul to the Christians coming from a pagan background and those of Peter to Jewish Christians. It could not be in any other way. The critics who place Peter in Rome forget that in order to be a leader, one must speak and how was an illiterate Jew to speak to the Romans? In what language?

The Church of Rome declares that its mandate originated in Jesus and in Peter, and that such a mandate reaches the whole world. Nevertheless, such a mandate never existed and Peter was never there. In addition, Paul in his letter to the Romans mentions a Christianity pre-existent in Rome, previous to him and Peter if we were to accept that Peter was there.

Definitely, the Roman Catholic Church and its power derive from the Roman Empire, which although adverse at the beginning became favorable later on, and the Bishop of Rome --probably starting with Julius I-- from the year 337 on, was adopting all the prerogatives from the old emperors, mainly their authority, paraphernalia, magnificence and luxury such as the triple crown called the "tiara", all of which has nothing to do with Jesus and his preaching of poverty and humility but all the opposite. Jesus never ever wore royal robes and crowns or silk gowns and tailored silky dresses. More than this, He openly declared that he did not even have a rock on which to rest his head. Later we shall study this evolution of power of the bishop of Rome. Furthermore, and against Jesus' practice, and as a result of the struggle for power, women were to be left out from the church ministry, hierarchy, and all the ecclesiastical high administrative positions. To be more certain, Mary Magdalene was declared a "prostitute" and later a repentant prostitute until today. Later, we shall try to discover who started the theory on the Roman supremacy in Christendom.

Chapter III

Peter in the Book of *Acts of the Apostles*

The study of Peter as he appears in the most important part of the New Testament, the four Gospels, has been completed. Now, the following book -the **Acts of the Apostles** (Ancient Greek: Πράξεις τῶν Ἀποστόλων, *Práxeis tôn Apostólōn*, Latin: Āctūs *Apostolōrum*, often referred to as **Acts**) will be examined. It is the fifth book of the New Testament, where we find the life of Christianity in its earlier moments and the roles of Peter and Paul in those days.

Acts and the Gospel of Luke make up a two-part work, Luke-Acts, by the same anonymous author, usually dated to around 80-90 CE. The first part, the **Gospel of Luke**, tells how God fulfilled his plan for the world's salvation through the life, death and resurrection of Jesus of Nazareth, the promised Messiah. **The Book of Acts** continues the story of Christianity in the first century, beginning with the Ascension of Christ. The early chapters, set in Jerusalem, describe the Day of Pentecost (the coming of the Holy Spirit) and the growth of the church in Jerusalem. Initially, the Jews were receptive to the Christian message, but soon they turned against the followers of the Messiah. Rejected by the Jews, the message is taken to the Gentiles. The later chapters tell of Paul's conversion, his mission in Asia Minor and the Aegean region, and finally his imprisonment in Rome, where he awaits trial.[11]

The first mention of Peter appears in chapter one, verse thirteen, as follows:

> *Then the apostles returned to Jerusalem from the hill called the Mount of Olives, a Sabbath day's walk from the city. After arriving, they went upstairs to the room where they were staying. Those present were Peter, John, James, Andrew, Philip, Thomas, Bartholomew, Matthew, James (son of Alphaeus), Simon the Zealot, and Judas (son of James). They all joined together constantly in prayer, along with the women and Mary the mother of Jesus, and with his brothers.*

After this indirect mention of Peter, the author of this book focuses directly on him at the moment in which he addresses a speech to the public; he makes two main fundamental points: a) Judas the traitor, the money he received for his treason, his horrible end, and the need to appoint a replacement; b) this replacement was to be selected from among the disciples who had accompanied Jesus from the moment of His baptism by John. They drew lots and Matthias was elected as one of the twelve apostles. It is obvious that they wished to maintain the number twelve selected by Jesus. Peter does not act as a leader or director in any of these procedures.

In numerology, twelve is the number of social perfection: twelve were the tribes of Israel, twelve the apostles selected by Jesus, twelve the thrones in which the disciples were to sit down, etc. Twelve times

---

[11] The preceding information on the Luke/Acts- two parts work has been taken from Wikipedia on the Internet.

twelve are one hundred-forty-four; one hundred-forty-four- thousand were the triumphant followers of the Lamb in the Apocalypse.[12]

The chapter II centers on the day of Pentecost.[13] They were all together in one place. Suddenly a sound like the blowing of a violent wind came from heaven and filled the whole house where they were sitting. They saw what seemed to be tongues of fire that came to rest on each of them, and they were filled with the Holy Spirit and began to speak in other tongues as the Spirit enabled them. (Acts 2: 1-4). Those who were around and did not understand anything commented that the disciples were drunk. This situation provided the occasion for the second speech of Peter, a superb piece in which he took advantage of the opportunity to blame the Jews for the death of Jesus and, at the same time, explained with a great number of quotes from the Old Testament the historical symbolism of King David. God had established Lord and Christ the very same Jesus that they had crucified, and resurrected on the third day, a fact/witnessed by himself and the apostles. Peter quoted a beautiful passage from the prophet Joel in which referring to the last days, the prophet says: *"Your sons and daughters will prophesy, your old men will dream dreams, your young men will see visions."* (Joel 2:28) The Latin translation also

---

[12] In numerology, One is the absolute; it does not have anything in which to reflect Itself except its own. This reflection, or expression of the One is also absolute and it is the Two. Now, they are two and, thus, Relation is established: the Relation of the One and the Two, which is also absolute, and we have the Three, which is absolute as well. This absolute Trinity creates the earth and man, who is the Fourth. Four are the cardinal points; forty the years of the people of Israel in the desert, etc. Three and four are seven, which is the number of individual perfection: seven are the cardinal virtues, seven the capital sins, seven are the sacraments, etc. Six is the number of imperfection: it is the closest to perfection but does not reach it. This is worse than not having approached it at all. This six, repeated absolutely (three times), 666, is the absolute imperfection, the number of the Beast in the last book of the Bible, the Apocalypses.

[13] It means fifty. It was an old festivity which was celebrated fifty days after Passover, in memory of the delivery of the Tables of the Law which God gave Moses on the Sinai Mountain. It is also the thanksgiving day for the harvest. In Christianity, it is the celebration the 50th day after Easter.

sounds very beautiful: *Juvenes vestri visiones videbunt et senes vestri somnia somniabunt.*

Peter's speech produced the amazing result of three thousand conversions - the first new Christians registered by history, about whom the biblical text gives a memorable reference:

> *They devoted themselves to the apostles' teaching and to fellowship, to the breaking of bread, and to prayer. (...) All the believers were together and had everything in common. They sold property and possessions to give to anyone who had need. (...) They broke bread in their homes and ate together with glad and sincere hearts, praising God and enjoying the favor of all the people. And the Lord added to their number daily those who were being saved.*
> (Acts 2: 42-47)

Chapter III presents another speech by Peter, rich in quotations from the Old Testament, in which he emphasizes Jesus' resurrection, delivered right after he and John cured a man crippled from birth. Immediately after, the priests arrived accompanied by the temple's captain and the Sadducees who were furious because of Peter's preaching on the resurrection. They threw them in jail. This time, the number of people converted by Peter's speech was almost five thousand.

Peter and John had to appear before the Jewish authorities and Peter took advantage of this occasion to preach to these authorities as well. It seems important to quote his words as recorded in the book of Acts 4:8-12:

> *Then Peter, filled with the Holy Spirit, said to them, "Rulers of the people and elders of Israel: If we this day are judged for a good deed done to a helpless man, by what means he has been made well, let it be known to you all, and to all the people of Israel, that by the name of Jesus Christ of Nazareth, whom you crucified, whom*

God raised from the dead, by Him this man stands here before you whole. This is the 'stone which was rejected by you builders, which has become the chief cornerstone. Nor is there salvation in any other, for there is no other name under heaven given among men by which we must be saved."

Notice that the very same Peter is the one who declares that the only fundamental rock of Christianity is Jesus, and Jesus alone! In addition, to be an apostle is equal to being a preacher of Jesus' and beyond this, there is no salvation. There are no saints, no holy virgins, no popes or Vaticans. Jesus is the only rock of salvation and He is to be with us **"until the end of time**." (Matthew 28:20).

Chapter Four concludes with asserting the theme of being a Christian. What is the essence of being a Christian? (Acts 4:32-35):

All the believers were one in heart and mind. No one claimed that any of their possessions was their own, but they shared everything they had. With great power the apostles continued to testify to the resurrection of the Lord Jesus. And God's grace was so powerfully at work in them all that there were no needy persons among them. For from time to time those who owned land or houses sold them, brought the money from the sales and put it at the apostles' feet, and it was distributed to anyone who had need.

Chapter Five narrates the regrettable Saphira and Ananias episode and the hard attitude of Peter vis a vis the partial retention of the money produced by the sale of a property which had been offered to the community. Immediately after, the apostles enter the scene performing a great number of miracles to the point that people were looking for at least Peter's shadow in order to be cured from their diseases. Due to this popularity and to their preaching the name of Jesus and His resurrection, the high priest and the Sadducees had them imprisoned but the angel of the Lord by night opened the prison doors, and brought them forth, and said: "Go, stand and speak in the temple to the people all the words of this life". (Acts 5: 19-20)

Right after, the High Priest finds them preaching and again forbids them to do so but Peter answers: *We ought to obey God rather than men.* (Acts 5:29). The chapter ends with Gamaliel's advice: let the apostles go in peace; if their activities were only human endeavors, very soon they will disappear but if from God, it would be impossible to destroy them and the Jewish authorities will finally end fighting against God (Acts 5: 38-39).

Chapter Six is very important in reference to Peter's position in the Church. Roman Catholics affirm that Peter was the chief of the Church, appointed by Jesus Christ Himself. Nevertheless, the New Testament (word of God according to the same church) shows him receiving orders from the Apostles and the Church Assembly as seen in Acts 6: 2-6 where the deaconate for the service of the Church is created:

> So, the Twelve gathered all the disciples together and said, "It would not be right for us to neglect the ministry of the word of God in order to wait on tables. Brothers and sisters, choose seven men from among you who are known to be full of the Spirit and wisdom. We will turn this responsibility over to them, and will give our attention to prayer and the ministry of the word." This proposal pleased the whole group. They chose Stephen, a man full of faith and of the Holy Spirit; also Philip, Procorus, Nicanor, Timon, Parmenas, and Nicolas from Antioch, a convert to Judaism. They presented these men to the apostles, who prayed and laid their hands on them.

It is more than evident that the apostles and the Church Assembly were in power and they decided what was to be done. The rest of this chapter and the following one narrate the activity of Stephen, one of the deacons just appointed. Chapter Eight initiates Paul who, before his conversion and under the name of Saul *"began to destroy the church. Going from house to house, he dragged off both men and women and put them in prison".* Starting at verse fourteen, Peter returns: *When the apostles in Jerusalem heard that Samaria had accepted the word of God, they sent Peter and John to Samaria. When they arrived, they prayed for the new believers there so that they might receive the Holy Spirit.*

Again, it is not Peter who commands and sends but he is commanded and sent and not alone but with another apostle.

The larger part of Chapter Nine refers to Saul and his conversion in Paul, the apostle to the gentiles. The chapter ends with the narration of two miracles made by Peter in Lydda and in Jaffa respectively.

Chapter Ten continues describing Peter's activity in Jaffa, specifically his encounter with the Centurion Cornelius which ends with the baptism of all in his house and his vision of food and the lesson given to him by a vision: *"What God has made clean, you have no right to call profane".* (Acts 10:15). This chapter is very important because it signals the aperture of God's church to all men of good will, not only to the Jews.

Chapter Eleven presents Peter's problem for entering a house of gentiles and eating non-kosher food. Peter defended himself by explaining the circumstances mentioned in the previous chapter. This section also has a central significance due to its clear derogation of all Jewish legalistic prescriptions and its affirmation of Christian liberty in the Lord.

Barnabas was sent from the church in Jerusalem to the church in Antioch probably to find out about these new happenings. Barnabas, extremely satisfied, also preached the name of the Lord and the result of his words was a new multitude added to the number of the believers. Then, Barnabas went to Tarsus to pick up Saul and brought him to Antioch, where they stayed a whole year.

It was here, in Antioch, that the believers began to be called "Christians". The chapter ends with the report of the money collected by the brethren in Antioch to help the people of Judea, money which was delivered directly to the local elders.

Again, it is highly important to notice that the local Christian churches, which were starting here and there, were ruled by local committees of "elders". There was no Peter or any delegate of his performing anything.

The martyrdom of Jacob, John's brother, follows as the first casualty of King Herod's persecution of the early Church. Peter ends up in jail but is freed by an angel. After killing the guards who were to keep Peter in custody, King Herod dies eaten away by worms.

Later, the elders of Antioch sent Barnabas and Saul on a first missionary trip. Most of chapter thirteen narrates the speech of Paul in Antioch of Pisidia and its results. Immediately after, a new chapter, Chapter Fourteen, describes the activities of Paul and Barnabas in Iconium, Lystra, Lycaonia and Derbe, and concludes with the end of first apostolic trip.

Chapter Fifteen has a foremost importance since it renders the first Christian Universal Council. Since many gentiles had become Christians, an argument started whether they were to be circumcised and instructed to keep the Law of Moses as the Jews were. Paul and Barnabas went up to Jerusalem (notice: "went to Jerusalem") to present these questions to the Apostles and the elders. After an initial discussion in which Peter, Barnabas, Paul, and James exposed their reasons, James who presided the meeting closed the session by stating:

> *It is my judgment, therefore, that we should not make it difficult for the Gentiles who are turning to God. Instead we should write to them, telling them to abstain from food polluted by idols, from sexual immorality, from the meat of strangled animals and from blood.* (Acts 15:19-20)

After this resolution, the apostles and the elders wrote the information as follows:

> *So we all agreed to choose some men and send them to you with our dear friends Barnabas and Paul—men who have risked their lives for the name of our Lord Jesus Christ. Therefore, we are sending Judas and Silas to*

confirm by word of mouth what we are writing: "It seemed good to the Holy Spirit and to us not to burden you with anything beyond the following requirements: You are to abstain from food sacrificed to idols, from blood, from the meat of strangled animals and from sexual immorality. You will do well to avoid these things. Farewell!" So, the men were sent off and went down to Antioch, where they gathered the church together and delivered the letter. The people read it and were glad for its encouraging message. (Acts 15: 25-31)

Once the message was delivered, Paul and Barnabas remained in Antioch for a while and preached the name of the Lord Jesus. Afterwards, they separated. Barnabas went to Cyprus and Paul to Syria and Cilicia consolidating the churches.

Thus, Chapter Fifteen ends and, with it, Peter also disappears; his name is not mentioned any more in the book of Acts.

Those who say that Peter was the chief of the church will do well reading these biblical chapters, mainly the Fifteenth, instead of going around writing nonsense on the Internet and making intentional "mistakes".

This book of the Acts of the Apostles has a total of twenty-eight chapters, the last thirteen dedicated to Paul. As it is absolutely clear in this first Christian historical account, the churches --not "the Church"-- were governed by committees of Elders, who made decisions by openly discussing the issues and, after arriving at conclusions, shared them with the others. Peter disappeared right here and we cannot know anything about his later doings.

Did he ever go to Rome? Was he the chief the Roman church? To begin with, as we have seen, there were no chiefs of churches but assemblies of elders ("presbiteroi" in the original Greek of the New Testament books). Then, in the second step, we should remember that Peter does not appear in Paul's letter to the Romans. There is no Peter there! The only place he shows up in the New Testament in addition to what we have seen here, is the letter of Paul to the Galatians, in which he is not chief of anything!!!

The solemn declaration by the Church of Rome that Peter was the first bishop there is impossible to defend as well as its right to the Apostolic Authority. There was no apostolic authority or an apostolic "commander" in the early church, as we have just seen! The Romans base their affirmation on no evidence at all. The evidence they proclaim simply does not exist; it is only noise of words. In addition, the "columns" of the Church, as Paul said, were not in Rome but in Jerusalem. Christianity originated not in Rome but in Jerusalem. Jesus was Jewish, the apostles were Jewish. Christianity was Jewish. Rome was the enemy which had conquered and occupied the land of the "chosen people". How and when Christianity became Roman? We shall see it later.

Chapter IV

Peter in the Letters of Paul

Section One: The Letters of Paul

The letters of Paul also known as "Pauline Epistles" are a set of fourteen letters authored by Paul or attributed to him, written in the first century from which we have copies as old as Papyrus P46 from 175-225[14]. These letters were accepted by all Christian churches and are a necessary source for the study of Christianity. They subdivide into two groups: 1) the "authentic epistles" which have Saint Paul as their almost certain author, 2) the "pseudo-epigraphic" which the contemporary critics consider written by other authors, associated with Paul.

Regarding the chronology of Paul's letters, the scholars divide them into four sections, as follows: 1) Early Epistles: First and Second Thessalonians; 2) The Great Epistles: First and Second Corinthians, Galatians, Romans, and possibly Philippians; 3) Captivity Epistles: Colossians, Ephesians (authorship disputed) and Philemon; 4) Pastoral Epistles (authorship extremely doubtful) First and Second Timothy and Titus.

1. Letter of Paul to the Galatians

Following the arrangement of the New Testament books, we shall now study how Peter appears in the letters of Paul. We only have one

---

[14] P46 is the earliest among the existent papyri from Paul's letters. It is kept in the Chester Beatty Library in Dublin, Ireland, and in the University of Michigan Library at Ann Arbor. This manuscript is extremely important to understand the transmission and first stages of Paul's writings.

letter in which Paul extensively mentions Peter, and it is <u>Galatians</u>. On his second and third trip, Paul wrote to the churches of Galatia because of the intervention of some other Christian missionaries still under the influence of Judaism in the churches he had founded during the last years of the forties in the Roman province of Galatia, in the center of Asia Minor (today Turkey) in the cities of Licaonia, Iconio, Listra, Derbe, and Antioch of Pisidia.

Christians who were still under the influence of Judaism mentioned salvation by the works of the Law and even required circumcision. Saint Paul received this information while possibly in Ephesus between the years 49 and 55. Immediately, he wrote a letter in which he appears irritated to the point of saying that *"even if I myself or an angel from Heaven would preach a different gospel from the one I have announced to you, be anathema!!!*, and adds: *I want you to know, brothers and sisters, that the gospel I preached is not of human origin. I did not receive it from any man, nor was I taught it; rather, I received it by revelation from Jesus Christ.*

His main doctrine is that man obtains salvation by means of faith in Jesus and not by the works of the Law. (Gal. 1: 8-12).

His mention of Peter happens in verse 18: *"Then, after three years, I went up to Jerusalem to get acquainted with Cephas and stayed with him fifteen days. I saw none of the other apostles—only James, the Lord's brother. (...).* And goes on: *"My trip was caused by a revelation and I exposed to them the Gospel I preach among the gentiles, although only to the most authorized, to avoid running in vain. (Gal 2: 1-2).*

The reason for which Paul wished to see Peter follows from the previous section, Chapter Ten of the book of Acts: Peter was the first to open Christian preaching to the Gentiles, forced by the insistence of the pious Roman centurion, who even compelled him to come to his house. For this same reason, Peter had problems for having entered a house of Gentiles and having eaten non kosher food.

The main cause for the trip of Paul to Jerusalem was to interview the apostles, the original leaders of the Christian community. The principal was James, the brother of Jesus, who was in charge of the group after the death of his brother. Fourteen years later, Paul returned to Jerusalem accompanied by Barnabas and Titus, probably to present these fellow workers coming from Gentility to the original leaders.

Notice that Jerusalem was the center of the Christian church.

The text which follows is too important to leave inside the paragraph. It is necessary to transcribe it apart and in italics because here we clearly see the mission of Peter in the Church. (Gal 2: 3-10):

> *Yet not even Titus, who was with me, was compelled to be circumcised, even though he was a Greek. This matter arose because some false believers had infiltrated our ranks to spy on the freedom we have in Christ Jesus and to make us slaves. We did not give in to them for a moment, so that the truth of the gospel might be preserved for you. As for those who were held in high esteem—whatever they were makes no difference to me; God does not show favoritism—they added nothing to my message. On the contrary, they recognized that I had been entrusted with the task of preaching the gospel to the uncircumcised just as Peter had been to the circumcised. For God, who was at work in Peter as an apostle to the circumcised, was also at work in me as an apostle to the Gentiles. James, Cephas and John, those esteemed as pillars, gave me and Barnabas the right hand of fellowship when they recognized the grace given to me. They agreed that we should go to the Gentiles, and they to the circumcised. All they asked was that we should continue to remember the poor, the very thing I had been eager to do all along.*

In this fragment from Galatians, we find all the answers for the fundamental questions of this study, mainly Peter's role in the initial church. There is no Rome, no popes, nothing of the paraphernalia with which later the Romans enriched themselves. The specific field of each one of them is clearly marked: James, Peter, and John would go to preach in the Jewish field and Paul would go the Pagans.

This decision was more than obvious and logical. Paul was a Greek by birth and his native language was Greek. The other three were Jewish, they spoke only Aramaic; they were not able to speak or write any language outside Israel, mainly Peter of whom the Bible itself declares that he was illiterate (Acts 4:13).

The chapter two of this letter concludes with the incident of Antioch. We do not know the motive for which Peter traveled to Antioch. Since in that city there were Christians previously baptized by Paul, Peter was invited and ate with them with the liberty of true Christians. At the same time, a few disciples of James traveled to Antioch; when Peter discovered it, he withdrew and abstained from sharing the table with those Christians[15]. Several among his companions did the same thing; even Barnabas allowed himself to be convinced. Paul got upset; he himself declares it in reference to Peter (Gal. 2:11):

> **"But when Peter came to Antioch, I had to oppose him to his face for what he did was very wrong"** *For before certain men came from James, he was eating with the Gentiles; but when they came he drew back and separated himself, fearing the circumcision party. And the rest of the Jews acted hypocritically along with him, so that even Barnabas was led astray by their hypocrisy. But when I saw that their conduct was not in step with the truth of the gospel, I said to Cephas before them all, "If you, though a Jew, live like a Gentile and not like a Jew, how can you force the Gentiles to live like Jews?"*

The lesson Peter learned is very clear; he has been a hypocrite and with his behavior he was contradicting the Christian message. Even worse, with regard to Christian Doctrine, he was inducing to error those Christians with whom he was dealing. This was precisely the reason for the strong reaction of Paul.

---

[15] This text confirms that James, Jesus' brother, was the head of the initial Christian group.

It is regrettable to find people who still today affirm that Peter was the chief. Chief of what? In Paul's letter, it clearly appears that Peter was one of the apostles, an important one, but not the first or one invested with a Primacy, or the chief of what later was created for political reasons that had nothing to do with Jesus and his doctrine.

In addition, notice that Peter reserved himself for the apostolate among the Jewish people which was the only thing he could do. Placing him in Rome without knowing Latin or Greek is simply an absurdity.

Many writers who consider themselves "critics" affirm that Paul did not mention Peter in his letter to the Romans because they did not coincide in time. The real reason is very different. Simply, Peter was never in Rome. Consider the following: a) preaching in Rome implied speaking to the gentiles which was Paul's domain according to the agreement. b) acting and living in Rome required speaking Latin or Greek, languages that Peter, the fisherman, ignored completely. The Bible itself says that Peter was illiterate as we have mentioned before.

2. Paul's letter to the Romans

Since it was attempted to associate Peter with Rome, let's examine the letter of Paul to the Romans in which there is not even a remote mention of Peter, and in addition, its doctrinal nucleus does not coincide with Peter's preaching as we have hinted in the Letter to the Galatians.

Paul wrote to the Romans during his third trip, probably during his stay in Corinth, at the beginning of the year 58 by using a scribe named Tertius, who took advantage of his job to add his personal greetings as well (Rom. 16:22). Paul had never been in Rome but considering that the majority of people in the city was pagan, he thought that he should preach there according to the agreement established with the apostles. For this reason and as a first step, Paul wrote the letter to the Romans, that a deaconess of the church of Cenchreae, named Phebe, brought personally to Rome. Paul traveled in person three years later. (Rom. 16: 1)

His main objective was to give the Pagans a systematic exposition of the Gospel's universal application, a solid and definitive theological treatise as a foundation of the Christian faith whose central theme is salvation through the faith in Jesus Christ, dead and resurrected; a salvation which is offered to all without any discrimination.

The letter also quotes the old prophecies. Obviously, the Christian Congregation of Rome was formed with Jews and Gentiles. Although Paul did not know them personally, very probably he received information about them from two co-workers, Priscila and Aquila, whom he also mentions. Judging by the salutation in Chapter 16, we can conclude that Paul knew some of the members. The majority were of Pagan background; the rest, Jewish. This fact caused tensions especially from the continuous incoming of new members from Pagan origin; tensions which were threatening the unity of the church.

The theological heart of the letter's exposition departs from the principle that the world is dominated by the power of **sin** which in multiple forms enslaves the humans and brings them to destructive and undignified behavior. Vis a vis this reality, the laws and the rituals are inefficient since the only solution resides in the internal liberation of man which is obtained by the faith in Jesus Christ dead and resurrected. Thanks to this faith, God liberates us from sin, death, and the law, and -in this way- man may advance in a new life, guided by the Spirit.

Paul does not use the word "salvation", but "justification", or "make us just". In biblical language "justice of God" is all what God wishes to effect in men: internal liberation, forgiveness, peace, and love. This is the real meaning of the word "holiness". Faith is not only the intellectual act of believing that God exists but, fundamentally, the adhesion of the whole person to the will and the word of God which are present in Jesus Christ.

The authenticity of this letter is very well established and its antecedents go back to an old and famous canon from year 170, known as Cannon Muratori.

Notice as well that this letter reveals a Christian organization existing in Rome before the arrival of Paul. It is impossible to know who established it there. Paul mentions congregations functioning in homes of women; he cites them in detail. And there is no mention of Peter whatsoever.

For all these reasons it is impossible to understand the big noise that the Vatican makes about the founders of the Church of Rome: "Saint Peter and Saint Paul". (????????) There is something very important that is called "politics"...... In this case, corrupt politics since it is based on lies.

3. **First Letter to the Corinthians**

It is very interesting to notice that in the first letter to the Corinthians, when Paul mentions the dissensions that occurred among Christians: "*I am of Paul, I of Apollo, I of Kephas, I of Christ ...*" (1Cor 1:12), already existed a Peters' party (Kephas)which the apostle does not doubt to condemn together with other Christian leaders, possible origin of schisms in the Church; schisms which certainly occurred later due to the pretensions of the Romans to conform the Church of Jesus to the lineaments of the Roman Empire.

At the same time, this letter contains another mention of Peter but in the Aramaic version of Kephas. It happens in chapter 9, verse 5. Saint Paul had been attacked by other Christians, and in this section of this letter he takes advantage to defend himself with the known text: "*Do we not have the right to take along a believing wife, as do the other apostles and the brothers of the Lord and Kephas?*" (I Cor. 9:5)

Some biblical commentators wish to interpret this text as if Paul would claim the right of having with him a Christian girl as a helper. Nevertheless, this is a wrong translation because the words used by Paul are "gynaika adelfe" which mean "Christian wife". "Adelfe" means a "sister", sister in the faith, and "Gynaika" means literally "wife" and not simply "girl", as Paul himself used the word a few lines before, when mandating that the husbands do not dismiss the wives (kai andra gynaika me apsienai) (chapter 7:11) as in many other passages of the same letter. This is to say that the Apostle claims "the right to take with him a "Christian wife as the apostles and the brothers of Jesus." About Peter, we already know that he had a wife since Jesus cured his mother in law (Math. 8:14-15). It is probable that Paul has mentioned Peter first because everybody knew from the beginning that he was married.

Later, in chapter fifteen, verse five, Paul mentions Peter again under the name Kephas when he says:

> *and that he appeared to Kephas, and then to the Twelve. After that, he appeared to more than five hundred of the brothers and sisters at the same time, most of whom are still living, though some have fallen asleep. Then he appeared to James, then to all the apostles, and last of all he appeared to me also, as to one abnormally born.*

It is not shown in the gospels that Peter would have received a special apparition from the resurrected Jesus. As we have studied before in the Gospel of Matthew, Jesus appeared first to Mary Magdalene and the other Mary; in Mark, to Mary, the Magdalene; in Luke, only to two disciples who were going to Emmaus; and in John, to Mary Magdalene alone. Paul definitely excludes the women in relation to Jesus; nevertheless, in his letter to the Romans, he was the first who mentioned the presence of women among the early Christians, up to nine women who took care of the Church or were related to it.

Any way, it looks like, contrary to Jesus' practices and teachings, the policy of maintaining women out of the officialdom of the church was official; a practice that comes to us from the very early days. As a matter of fact, the Roman Catholic Church excludes women up to this day. It prevents them from becoming ministers, bishops, cardinals, and —of course- popes, and very solemnly declares that Jesus so commanded it.

As a matter of fact, this is exactly what Paul declares in this letter to the Romans when he refers to women, as he does in the Epistle to the Ephesians as well, where he commands them to be strictly subjects to their husbands; the same as in Colossians, the same as in

Timothy. Paul never mentioned Mary Magdalene or the other women beloved by Jesus.

Returning to our topic, the other Pauls' Authentic Epistles entirely omit the mention of Peter. The same thing we find in the Deutero-Pauline epistles: there is not even a tiny mention of Peter. At the same time, Paul never told the churches that they were to be submitted to other more important or powerful churches. There was perfect equality among all the churches, submitted equally and only to the Lordship of Jesus Christ.

Chapter Five

The Epistles of Peter, the Catholic Epistles, and the Apocalypse

Before any other consideration, we should remember what we have already explained: that the word "peter" does not exist in the ancient texts; it is a word created in the Middle Ages for the English language in order to translate the word "petros" which literally means "stone"; a nickname that Jesus gave to Simon when He called him to become an apostle.

The Letters of Peter

The Apostle Peter wrote two epistles, which we may call "circular letters", addressed to the Christians who came from Judaism, and were dispersed throughout the areas of Ponto, Galatia, Cappadocia, Asia, and Bitinia. These five places were in a region called Asia Minor, today Turkey. The first letter opens with a brief introductory salutation followed by a few exhortations to improve Christian life vis a vis the imminent end of all things.

As Jesus did, Peter's preaching intensively recommended to be prepared for the arrival of the Kingdom, which is already at the doors. He uses metaphors frequently employed by Jesus and the apostles such as *"all flesh is like grass…"* (I Peter 1:24) Among the symbols preferred by Peter, the "stone" or the "rock" stands out. See in particular chapter two of this letter, in which Peter goes back to the prophet Isaiah in order to find a prophecy referring to the appearance of Jesus the Christ: *"See, I lay a stone in Zion, a tested stone, a precious cornerstone for a sure foundation; the one who relies on it will never be lost"* (Is. 28:16). In the same way, Paul does it in his letter to the Romans. See chapter nine, verse thirty-three: *"See, I lay in Zion a stone that causes people to stumble and a rock that makes them fall, and the one who believes in him will never be put to shame."*

It is obvious that the apostles considered the stone an efficient symbol to represent Jesus. Let's now read from Peter as he expresses himself in reference to this point:

> *As you come to him, the living Stone—rejected by humans but chosen by God and precious to him—you also, like living stones, are being built into a spiritual house to be a holy priesthood, offering spiritual sacrifices acceptable to God through Jesus Christ. For in Scripture it says: "See, I lay a stone in Zion, a chosen and precious cornerstone, and the one who trusts in him will never be put to shame." Now to you who believe, this stone is precious. But to those who do not believe, "The stone the builders rejected has become the cornerstone," and, "A stone that causes people to stumble and a rock that makes them fall." They stumble because they disobey the message—which is also what they were destined for.*

The Gospel of Matthew had used the same symbol to refer to Jesus (Matthew 21:42): *Jesus said to them, "Haven't you ever read in the scriptures: The stone that the builders rejected has become the cornerstone".*

For this reason, the unknown Romans who dared to interpolate in Matthew 16: 18 the phrase *"And I tell you that you are Peter, and on this rock, I will build my church, (...)* took away from Jesus his function and character of cornerstone and foundation stone of the church in order to give it to a human being. Obviously, their reasons were political in order to place Rome at the top of Christianity, and degrade all the other churches. Furthermore, in addition to falsifying historical facts, they committed the worst sin of blasphemy in history.

Still, they created for themselves a more difficult task: to bring Peter to Rome and make him an "absolute" bishop when such a function did not exist yet and Peter had never stepped a foot in Italy. Also, they made Jesus appear to have wished to found a church when He had never said such a thing but the contrary: He always announced the end of everything.

Even more, by reading the original language, Greek, we can see an even bigger blunder: the word "church" in the original text is "εκκλησια" (ekklesia) and Jesus never ever could have said that; and this is the best proof of a later interpolation. "Ecclesia" was in those days a Greek, pagan and aristocratic organization, as we have explained before, and it is an absolute absurdity to assume that Jesus wished to found a pagan aristocratic society.

Finally, the writer of this Peter One letter does not forget women. He categorically mandates *"you, wives, should be obedient to your husbands"* (I Peter Chapter III, vers. 1-6), and repeats it again *"as the holly women of the past (...) were submissive to their husbands, like Sarah who was obedient to Abraham and called him 'her Lord'."*

In the second letter, Peter refers to teachers (II Peter 2: 12-22), of whom he says: *"false teachers"*, *"brute beasts, born only to be caught and killed and, like beasts, they will be destroyed. (...) with their eyes always looking for adultery, dumb beasts of burden (...) They may promise freedom but are themselves slaves (...) dried up springs, fogs swirling in the winds (...) high sounding but empty talk (...) They do as the proverb has rightly said: "The dog goes back to its vomit".*

After this chain of insults, the author returns to insist on the second coming of Jesus with which he ends his epistle.

The Catholic Epistles

The rest of the epistles, one from James, three from John and one from Judas have been called "catholic epistles" or universal letters although they addressed mainly to the Jewish world.[16]

---

[16] They also include the two from Peter, studied before.

a) Letter from James

The author calls himself "Jacob". He is the one we know under the name of James, the Minor, son of Alphaeus. He is the same person that Paul mentions as the brother of the Lord (Gal 1:19) and leader of the earliest Christian community in Jerusalem. In the Spanish Bibles he is called "Santiago", a name formed by the contraction of two words: Sant (Saint) + Iago (Jacob). The Gospel of Matthew (Chapter 13:55) reports that he was one of the brothers of Jesus: "*Is not his mother a woman called Mary and His brothers, James and Joseph, and Simon and Jude?*

The Greek text of this letter starts directly: "*From James, servant of God and of the Lord Jesus. Greetings to the twelve tribes of the dispersion.*" The main message in this letter is that faith should be shown by works. The coming of the Lord is imminent. It does not mention Peter.

b) Letters from John

They are three, one more general and important; the other two, very short. In the first letter, as Jesus preached, declares that the end of Time is near and the Antichrist is coming; in order to protect themselves, people of God should keep the commandments, especially that of love and be detached from the world. Above all, Christians should be aware of the Antichrist, and live as God's children, far from sin. **Love for God is shown in love for others.** The second letter of John is addressed to a Christian woman named Electa and her children to protect her against the false teachers. In the third letter, John praises a Christian named Gaius. The writer never mentions Peter.

c) The letter of Jude

It belongs to the youngest brother of Jesus. It is addressed to the Judeo-Christians and prevents them against the false teachers. It does not mention Peter.

The Apocalypse

The Book of Revelation or Apocalypse of Saint John (Αποκαλυψs Ιωαννου) is the last book of the New Testament. It is also known as *Revelations of Jesus/Christ*. Its author identifies himself as John, exiled in the island of Patmos, in the Aegean Sea, on account of the Word of God. (Apo. 1:9). Biblical commentators classify this work as written by the end of the first century or the beginning of the second when the Roman persecutions against Christians became more violent during the days of Emperor Diocletian.

It was accepted into de New Testament by a decree of Pope Damasus I, in the year 382 and confirmed later by the councils of Hippo in 393 and Carthage in 397. Its main objective coincides with the Catholic Epistles: to caution believers against the false prophets, who will be everywhere, in the last days. It does not mention Peter; on the contrary, to those who wish to triumphantly bring Peter to Rome, there are verses 16 and 17, in Chapter 18 which say: "*Mourn for this great city; for all the linen and purple and scarlet that you wore, for all your finery of gold and jewels and pearls; your huge riches are all destroyed within a single hour*".

Chapter VI

Other Ancient Documents Which Mention Peter

I. <u>The Gospel of Mary</u>

The Gospel of Mary is a Gnostic Apocryphal Gospel written between the years of 120 and 180. From this Gospel only three fragments are conserved; two are extremely short, in Greek, kept within manuscripts of the third century: *Papyrus Rylands* 463 and Papyrus Oxyrhyrinchus 3525. The third fragment is less brief, written in Coptic, *Berolinensis Gnosticus* 8052.1, probably a translation from a Greek original. The Coptic text was found in 1896 by Carl Schmidt although it was not published until 1955. The Greek fragments instead were available in print respectively in 1938 and 1983.

The author of this Gospel is totally unknown. It was probably composed in the Second Century. The name which this work traditionally receives, "Gospel of Mary Magdalene", is due to the fact that a disciple of Jesus named Mary is mentioned within the text. Several scholars identify her with the Mary Magdalene of the Canonic Gospels. This Mary appears in a close relationship with Jesus, and receives from Him a secret revelation.

The larger fragment, the one written in Coptic, is missing several pages in two sections: 1 through 6, and 11 through 14. The whole text consists of a long dialogue between Jesus, mentioned as "the Savior", His disciples, and a woman named "*Mariam*". It narrates that after Jesus' ascension, "*the disciples were extremely sad, and bitterly cried* saying: *'how are we going to the gentiles to preach the gospel of the Son of Man? If they had no consideration of Him how will they have it for us?'* Then, Mariam arose, greeted everybody, and said to them: *'Brethren, do not cry and do not be sad, do not hesitate any longer because His grace will descend upon you all and will protect you. Rather lets praise His greatness".* Mary succeeded and convinced them.

In summary, in the partial text that we possess, we see that the disciples had previously directed questions to the resurrected Christ. He answered them and right after sent the apostles to preach the *Gospel of the Kingdom* to the Gentiles, and ascended to Heaven. The disciples became sad, feeling incapable of fulfilling Jesus' request. Then, Mary managed to encourage them to carry out the Savior's command.

Then, Peter asked Mary to tell him and the whole group any message or revelation from the Savior that they may not know, since they all were aware that the Savior loved her more than all the other women. Mariam, then, narrated a vision she had of a world which was going to its dissolution and explained the difficulties of the soul to discover its true spiritual nature in its ascension to the place of its eternal rest.

When she finished her exposition, Andrew and Peter declared that they did not believe that Jesus would have had such a profound conversation with a woman. In addition, Peter refused to believe that the Savior would prefer her above the apostles. Mariam started to cry. Levi defended her, and told Peter: *"Peter, you always so impetuous!",* and blamed him for attacking Mariam as an enemy. He asked him to simply accept that the Savior preferred her above all women, and recommended all the apostles and disciples to put on the perfect man and go out to preach the gospel. Levi's strong words were addressed directly to Peter. The complete text is as follows:

> *"Peter, you have always anger on your soul and at this very moment you are arguing with Mariam confronting her. If the Savior had considered her worthy, who are you to despise her? He, the Savior, without any doubt, has loved*

> *her more than us. Let's rather be ashamed and coated*
> *the perfect man, let us fulfill what was commanded us.*
> *Let us preach the Gospel without restrictions and without*
> *legislating as the Savior said." As soon as Levi finished*
> *these words he left and started to preach the gospel.*

Then, all of them imitated him.

2. <u>The texts of Nag Hammadi</u>

The manuscripts of Nag Hammadi or *The Library of Nag Hammadi,* also known as the *Gnostic Gospels*[17] is a collection of texts which contain a series of writings from the early Christians, such as gospels, apocalypses, theological treatises, and words attributed to Jesus. They were discovered near a town called "Nag Hammadi" in Upper Egypt, in December of 1945. This library includes thirteen ancient leather-bound books (called "codices") written on papyrus, containing over fifty texts, among them a large number of "Gnostic Gospels", texts once thought to have been entirely destroyed during the early Christian struggle to define "orthodoxy". Among them, are standing the <u>Gospel of Thomas</u>, the <u>Gospel of Philip</u>, or the <u>Gospel of Truth</u>. All these documents were carefully placed in a ceramic jar sealed and deposited in a cave on the mountains of *Jabal al-Tari;* they were found by a farmer named Muhammad Ali al-Samman. They are written in Coptic between the centuries III and IV of the Christian Era. It is believed that the lost Greek originals had been completed by the Second Century.

The discovery and translation of the Nag Hammadi library has provided great impetus to a major re-evaluation of early Christian history and the nature of Gnosticism. These codices are now kept in the Coptic Museum of Cairo, Egypt.

---

[17] The Gnostics postulated a God impossible to be known. He is the absolute transcendence.

Note: for this section, we have followed the work "Textos Gnósticos" by Antonio Piñero, José Montserrat Torres, and Francisco García Bazán. Vols. I, II, and III. Madrid, Editorial Trotta, S.A., 1997, 1999,2000.

What we know now as "Nag Hammadi" was before "Xhnobockeion" where, in the year 320, Saint Pachomius had established the first Christian monastery. In the year 367 Saint Athanasius of Alexandria prohibited all scriptures not approved by the Central Church; now it is believed that this decree was the cause for some monks to copy those documents in the thirteen volumes and hide them in the rocks where they remained for one thousand six hundred years.

These manuscripts encompass fifty three Gnostic treatises, three works of the *Corpus Hermeticum*[18], and a partial translation of *The Republic* by Plato. They are not presented in the typical format of the ancient works, the rolls, but in the form of books whose pages allowed the writers to take advantage of both sides of the sheets, made with the expensive material of papyrus, with covers and strings made out of parchment.

They were published in 1984. This publication has allowed the researchers access to the most important source of information about Gnosticism. At the same time, it was discovered that some of their sections had already been found in previous manuscripts, found in 1898, in Oxyrhynchus[19], the ancient Egyptian city, today's El-Bahnasa., at about 160 km southwest of Cairo.

Another reason for which the texts of Nag Hammadi are important is that they had not been altered as the Bible was, and bring the thinking of their authors and their time directly to us. The only reason for which these documents are presented in this study is the mention of Peter, which happens in several sections.

---

[18] According to the tradition the Corpus was written by Hermes Trismegistus, originally a representation of the Egyptian god Thoth, that later was known as a wise man who in ancient times had founded the alchimia and other hermetic sciences. The works of Hermes Trismegistus, which were known with the generic name of "Hermetica", had a great influence in the development of the intellectual world of Renaissance.

[19] The list of codices may be found in Wikipedia: http://es.wikipedia.org

1. The Daughter of Peter

The first text which mentions Peter among the Nag Hammadi documents appears in the Codex VI, <u>Acts of Peter</u>, in which a short fragment titled *"The Daughter of Peter"* presents the apostle performing a great number of miracles by curing sick people, while in his own house he has a paralyzed daughter. People mentioned this strange fact to him and he decided to cure her as well. Everybody was pleased but Peter right away produced another miracle by which he made his daughter paralyzed again, in order to protect her from the dangers of her beauty. The ultimate theme of this text is that virginity is the ideal condition for people.

2. The Acts of Peter and the Twelve Apostles

Peter and his companions go out in order to preach the *Good News;* they take a boat and arrive on an island named "Inhabitation". There, Peter encounters a character named "Litargoel" who is a seller of pearls. The name of this man means "stone of special brightness, like a pearl". The man asks Peter to have the courage to go to the city although its road is difficult and dangerous. Later, Litargoel re-appears dressed as a physician. Finally, he reveals himself as Jesus. Peter and his companions adore him and proclaim themselves ready to fulfill His will although they have nothing to offer because they had renounced everything for Him. Jesus answers that they have the most important: His name, which is more powerful than anything else and with it they can cure all sick people, and curing the body is the first step to curing the soul. Finally, Jesus asks them to avoid any contact with the rich.

The doctrinal intention of this text is evident: the divine reality of Jesus and his quality as the Savior, the need to be firms in the faith, to be poor, to mortify the flesh, and turn away from worldly desires in order to acquire a place in the Kingdom of Heaven.

3. Letter from Peter to Philip

Peter asks Philip to reunite with him and his companions in the Mount of Olives. Then, Jesus appears to them, and they take advantage of this occasion to ask him questions such as: how did the deficiency of the "Eones" happen, since this is the cause for the human beings to be detained on Earth? How to break out? How to be able to speak with freedom and authority? The Savior answers in four points: 1) the origin of the deficiency originates in the fall of Wisdom; 2) the plenitude of the "Pleroma" resides in Jesus; 3) the retention on Earth is due to the envy and wickedness of the "Archontes", who rule the world; 4) the "Powers" attack the spiritual women and men because they belong to the Savior and are the People of Light.

Immediately after, the text presents a final question and its answer: How should we fight against the "Archontes"? The answer is: by means of the union of the brethren in the preaching of salvation and prayer, which obtains the strength of God.

The brethren return to Jerusalem, and Peter reminds them of Jesus' sufferings who descended to Earth and became like men. He died, resurrected and ascended to Heaven. Then, all of them request from the Savior the gift of "Spirit of Knowledge" and go out to preach. Jesus promises them His peace, His grace, and His power.

4. Apocryphal of James

Although this text does not refer to Peter directly, the main characters in addition to Jesus are, James and Peter. They witness the ascension of Jesus to Heaven and, later, inform the rest of the disciples about this fact and the promise of Life offered by Jesus. They also remind the disciples of the new ones who will come whom they should love in order to obtain salvation.

5. Apocalypse of Peter

In Codex VII a text appears which presents Peter receiving a special vision of Jesus during the Passion Week when Jesus was preaching in the temple before his imprisonment. The vision reviews the denials of Peter, and the crucifixion and resurrection of Jesus.

The resurrection is seen in Gnostic terms as a reunion of the spiritual body of Jesus with the intellectual light of the celestial "Pleroma".

It also denounces the adversaries: the ecclesiastic personnel. It declares: *"Others exist who do not belong to you and call themselves bishops and deacons as if they had received God's authority. They are under the judgment of the Principals. They are empty channels"*

The book concludes with Jesus' exhortations to Peter: *"You, be courageous and do not fear because I will always be with you so that your enemies will not have power on you. Peace be with you. Be strong!*

Final Considerations

Here, all references to Peter in the texts of Nag Hammadi conclude. Peter always appears as a calm and even-tempered man. He is not the impulsive and tendentious subject seen before in the previous texts. He is not in Rome or Head of any church or ecclesiastical institution.

Next, we will study the history of the first bishops of Rome in order to discover when and who created the legend of Peter in Rome and initiated the ambitious project of becoming his "successors", the Head of Christianity, and infallible source of all truth. We should keep in mind that in order to reach such an ambitious project it was necessary for whoever did it, to invent history and insert words within the text of the New Testament.

Chapter VII

The First Bishops of Rome[20]

Nobody knows who brought Christianity to Rome or who was its first bishop but it is certain that the first Christians appeared in Rome at a very early date. The *Epistle to the Romans* by Saint Paul is the first document which reveals a Christian group living in the city. Saint Paul wrote that letter while living in Corinth at the beginning of year 58, using the service of a copyist named "Tertius". A Christian woman named Phoebe, a deaconess in the church of Cenchrea, personally took it to the Romans (See Rom. 16.1). In this letter Paul does not mention any hierarchy or a bishop in Rome. Simply, he addressed his letter "to all who are in Rome" (Rom. 1:7). In chapter Sixteen, the last one in the letter, he greeted "all of you who are in Rome" without mentioning any bishop or presbyter[21]; he simply saluted and informed them that he had intentions to visit them in

---

[20] For the composition of this chapter, we have used several documents taken from the Internet, mainly www.centrorey.org *Historia de los Papas de Roma*. At the same time, we have reviewed Internet in reference to each of the Popes mentioned in this chapter.

[21] The "presbyter", (from Greek via Latin, a word which means "older". According to the Old Testament, they were leaders who operated as a council. In the New Testament, the word is used as a synonym of "Episcopos" (bishop) which means in Greek "the one who looks from above" (The same as the Latin word "Supervisor"). Later, after the death of the apostles the two words were used to mean different roles: Episcopos and Presbyters. The title of "bishop" does not appear until half of the Second Century, and the titles of "Pope" or "Pontifex Maximus" did not show up until the Fourth Century.

order to give them more information on the Gospel which they had believed in. (Rom. 1:9-13).

In the year 180, the bishop of Lyons (178-200), Saint Irenaeus, wrote the oldest known list of the Roman bishops. The name of Peter does not show up. It is also known that there was a leader of the Church of Rome named "Linus", who may have been a local presbyter. The earliest witness to Linus's status as bishop was Saint Irenaeus, who in about the year 180 wrote, "The blessed apostles, then, having founded and built up the Church, committed into the hands of Linus the office of the episcopate." The *Oxford Dictionary of Popes* presents Linus as the first bishop of Rome.

At the beginning, the bishop of any city was an elder (presbyter) who with other elders (presbyters) formed the government of a church which became established in any particular place. (Acts 14:23 and Titus 1:5) It was in the fourth century that the position of bishop acquired the character of a governor with all powers, according to the model of the Roman Empire.

Eusebius of Caesarea completed the first editions of his *Ecclesiastical History* and *Chronicle* before year 300. There he informs that the first bishop of Rome was Linus. He does not mention Peter or any Pope.

Before the fifth century, it was a generalized custom to apply to the bishops of every city the name of "father", (which in Greek is "Papas" and in English "Pope") as a loving appellative, not as a hierarchical title as it is done today, and even less as vicars of Christ. From the time of Emperor Constantine in the fourth century, the name of "*papas*" became a title given to the more politically important bishop of the Empire, this is to say Rome since it was the capital of the Empire.

In February of the year 313, Emperor Constantine published the Edict of Milan which decriminalized Christianity and gave great importance to a Christian group that today we call "*the proto-orthodox*". During the papacy of Sylvester I (314-335) the Council of Nicaea was gathered (325) which declared the divine nature of Jesus and the dogma of the most Holy Trinity against a much extended doctrine called "Arrianism". It was the Emperor who convened this fundamental council for Christianity, not the bishop of Rome and even more, from this time on, no Pope was elected without the Emperor's authorization.

After the death of Constantine, when Christianity became the "official religion", it became customary that the bishop of Rome, the Pope, was elected by the Emperor with the assistance of influential patrician families of Rome.

Thus, on February 6 of 337, Julius I, born in Rome, was elected Pope. One of his most important decisions was to support Athanasius (293-373), a very significant decision because this bishop was the one who had defended the true faith in the Council of Nicaea against the Arians, who denied the divine nature of Christ.

Julius took advantage of his first move to exalt the mission of the Papacy as Defender of Orthodoxy. In 342, he wrote a pastoral letter addressed to the eastern bishops, which is considered the first clear attempt of the Bishop of Rome to claim the "**Primacy**" over all other bishops. In addition, he quickly moved to put together another council in order to confirm his claim; a council which was finally gathered in Sardica (today's Sophia, Bulgaria) a few months later during the Fall of 343.

Regretfully, the result of this Council was the first schism between the Oriental and the Occidental sections of the Church, when the bishops of each side excommunicated each other without ever reaching an agreement. Julius had sent as his representatives two priests and a deacon -- Archidamus, Philoxenus, and Leo **respectively**. The bishops of the eastern side of the Empire were afraid of being a minority since they were only 76 men. For this reason, they vociferously withdrew, and organized a counter-synod in Philipppolis, which concluded deposing Julius. Meanwhile, the western side went -on and confirmed in the first place the innocence of Athanasius and his thesis on the divinity of Jesus, and established rules regarding how to proceed against bishops accused of doctrinal errors. The synod concluded recognizing the authority of the bishop of Rome, affirming at the same time the supreme power of the Pope.

He took advantage of it to declare: "*It cannot be ignored that in every question, it is necessary to come <u>to Us</u>* (that is to say, to him, Julius, speaking in majestic plural) *so that from here* (Rome) *be defined what is just*". This affirmation is considered the first declaration of the **Bishop** of Rome's primacy. Julius was also the first bishop of Rome who attributed himself the title of "Pope", which although still unusual in Occident, would succeed and finally be reserved exclusively for the bishop of Rome.

In the year 366, Damasus I was elected Pope but, at the same time, a rival party elected another candidate, Ursinus. The fight among both parties was armed and violent. Damasus defeated Ursinus in a bloody battle which lasted three days and left 130 men dead.

The church was by now a political power of significant influence in thousands of the Roman Empire citizens. The Emperors started to realize such a power and were looking for the manner to take it over. Pope Damasus on his part did the same thing, and worked intensively to increase the power of the Papacy. In the first place, he tried to get the power of the State to support and impose ecclesiastical decisions. Emperor Theodosius accepted it and in the year 380 ratified the alliance between the Empire and the Church by means of the Imperial Decree of February 28, which required that all subjects of the Empire should accept "*the religion of Peter*" of which Bishop Damasus of Rome was the depositary. This decree has been considered "*the foundation of the State Catholic Church*". Dave Hunt wrote: "*Dámasus was the first (in the year 382) to use the phrase "You are Peter, and on this rock, I will establish my church", in order to claim supreme spiritual authority. This bloodthirsty Pope, rich, powerful, and extremely corrupt surrounded himself with such a luxury that would have made feel shameful even an emperor. There is not a possible way to justify a comparison between him and Jesus Christ. Nevertheless, he is still mentioned as a link in the chain of the alleged succession of Peter.* ("A Woman Rides the Beast", p. 108). In this way, Damasus created the concept of "*Apostolic See*" or "*Holy See*" and was affirming the assimilation of the Pope's identity with that of Peter, and at the same time assured the primacy of Rome above all other Episcopal sees; a primacy which was finally officially declared by the Synod of Rome in the year 382.

Before leaving Pope Damasus, it is important to remember that he was the one who appointed as his secretary whom later was Saint Jerome, who sponsored the translation of the Bible into Latin, which was later known as the *"Vulgate"*. Around this time appeared in chapter sixteen of the Gospel of Matthew the phrase *"You are Peter and on this rock I will found my church"* ... We do not have proofs of anything else but is important to know this information.

The successor of Damasus was Siricius (384-399), who designed the "Decretal", a letter or rescript, that -since then- the bishops of Rome, living aside any fraternal or paternal approach, adopted as an official and authoritarian declaration like the imperial decrees.

His absolutist style is evident in his most famous document, a "decretal" addressed to bishop Himerius, from the Spanish church of Tarragona, in response to a nice letter that this bishop had sent to Damasus but had arrived in Rome after his death. There, Pope Siricius brusquely tells Himerius that he had found in his letter "things worth rebuke and correction"; mainly he emphasizes that he was the successor of Peter, blessed very specially by the apostle, *"who in everything protect us and preserve us from any evil since we are the **heirs of his administration**"*. He makes for Himerius a long list of prohibitions and finally orders him to inform his neighboring bishops *the statutes which soundly, prudently, and carefully we **have established***".

The pontificate of Siricius may be summarized as a constant effort to give the decisions of the Roman See a strict character of obligation.

Innocent I, Pope between 401 and 417, was born in Albano, the son of the previous Pope, Athanasius I. He commanded that any serious case was to be reviewed by him but since he did not define what was understood by the word "serious", he reserved for himself the right to get into anything that may call his attention. He used the "decretales" invented by Pope Siricius to extend the power of the Papacy.

Boniface I, Pope between 418 and 422, decreed that women, even the nuns, could not touch the sacred vestments or get near the altar. He introduced in the temples the Easter candles as the Pagans used to do, of whom Lactantius the apologist of the IV century had written: *"They light candles to God as if He lived in darkness. Do not deserve them to be considered as mentally insane for offering light to the creator of light?*

Things going on in this trend, in the year 431, with the occasion of the Council of Ephesus, the delegate sent by the Pope declared: *"Peter, Head of the apostles, column of the faith, and cornerstone of the Church, lives and judges today and forever in his successors".*

In the year 450, Leo I, Pope between 440 and 461, personally assumed the supremacy of Occident and adopted for himself the adjective of "Great" (Magnus) as if he was the emperor. He was the first Pope that required "plenitudo potestatis", this is to say "total power". After him, all bishops of Rome declared themselves "Heirs of Saint Peter".

The Imperial Rome was resurrecting now and imposing itself on the world by means of Peter's power as before it had done it by the sword. The same despotic spirit of the Imperial Rome was entering to stay in the Christian Rome in order to govern the world not in the name of a mortal emperor but in the sacred name of God, an infinite power that even in dreams the Imperial Rome could not conceive.

According to Pope Leo, the Roman Pontiff was above everything and everybody, and as God on earth, had the power to "tie and untie" according to his will. His will was the will of God!

This blasphemous principle was developing more and more forcefully during the run of the centuries until reaching its culmination in the Vatican I, a council called by Pope Pius IX, in the year 1869, which declared as "Dogma of Faith" nothing less than the doctrine of the <u>infallibility</u> of the Pope: the Pope was infallible!!!

It seems appropriate to study here as well the "tiara" and the "mitre" which are sort of crowns the Pope uses in all official ceremonies. Already starting in the fourth century, the Pope crowned himself with the "tiara" which was in the past a sign of distinction used by the Pagan priests from Persia and also the eastern emperors. According to Ralph Woodrow, *"the tiara used by the Popes, although decorated in different forms, is identical to the ones used by the gods that we can see in the Pagan documents of Assiria"*. By using this insignia, the Bishop of Rome intended to distinguish himself from the rest of the mortals, mainly from his colleagues, all the other bishops. At the time of its introduction, the tiara did not have any crown, as the tiaras of the Persian priests, but it changed through the years until acquiring the three crowns of today. This is the definition given by the Catholic encyclopedia: *"headdress worn by the pope, consisting of a beehive-shaped diadem surrounded by three coronets which symbolize his triple authority: spiritual authority over the souls, temporal authority over the Papal States and a mixed authority (spiritual and temporal) over all kings, presidents and powers of earth"*. (¿¿¿???) **Nothing less!!!**

The "mitre" has a similar origin; it is Pagan. It comes from the cult to Dagon, which had become popular among the idolater Philistines (See Judges 16:23 and I Samuel, chapter five). It imitates the head of a fish that the priest placed on his head while the rest of the fish body fell on his back like a cape. Later, this section was suppressed and only the head of the fish was used to ornate the head of the priest. This old Pagan "mitre" is the one used by the Pope and the bishops with the intention of impressing the faithful.

Never ever had Jesus or the apostles required the use of such costumes or used them, as Peter, the one they say was the first Pope, declared: *"Your beauty should not come from outward adornment, such as elaborate hairstyles and the wearing of gold jewelry or fine clothes. Rather, it should be that of your inner self, the unfading beauty of a gentle and quiet spirit, which is of great worth in God's sight."* (I Peter 3: 3-4)

At the same time, another factor was slowly invading Christianity: the cult of the saints and the Virgin Mary was replacing the Pagan gods as patrons of temples and cities. This Pope Leo boasted that Peter and Paul had replaced Romulus and Remo as **patrons** and protectors of Rome. What Pope Leo I really did was change the names of the Pagan gods and replace them with those of Christian saints.

Later, the Popes continued increasing their power by means of definite stages:

1) The first stage consisted of solemn declarations of universal dominion, such as the pronouncements of Boniface VIII who stated that Jesus gave His *bride,* the Church "*an absolute power so that she, the church, will be able to exercise its power on all the faithful*" (*Bulla Ineffabilis Amor,* 1296). Later, in 1302, the same Pope published the **Bulla Unam Sanctam**, solemnly declaring the Church has "two swords", one for spiritual items and the other for civilian affairs and for this same reason, the Church has authority over all governments either religious or civilian and for this reason anybody who put him/herself outside of the Papal authority was destined to **eternal damnation.** The Bulla Unam Sanctam truly established that all power of government has a divine origin and comes from God through the Pope. Notice the words "all power", including the civilian governments of all countries. It also added that the punishment for resisting the Pope goes beyond death and the tomb, it belongs to the dominion of the eternal life and salvation!

2) The second stage was terror. The Roman popes fortified their authority by adding fear and terror to their declarations; they established the famous "Inquisition" in both continents, Europe and **America**, with sufficient authority to condemn anybody who not only refused but even doubted of their "divine" power This condemnation was the worst that any human imagination could conceive: a horrible death in which the accused, man or woman, was slowly burned alive tied to a stake. (Certainly diabolical!) This terror lasted for more than six hundred years until Emperor Napoleon abolished the Inquisition, although terror persisted and was always favored by the Church of Rome, at least psychologically.

3) The third stage was acting and proceeding as if the Popes of Rome really had the power of a ferocious and vindictive God,

condemning, cursing, and excommunicating with efficient strength in the times in which the Christian countries believed in such a power.

4) The fourth stage began with the Popes of the Renaissance, starting with Julius II in 1506, who discovered that solemn declarations, terror and divine fury were not the main source of power. Luxury, greatness, and magnificence were! Thus, the great Basilica of Saint Peter was born in the heart of the Vatican. It was conceived to be the greatest and more luxurious church of Christendom. Then, in the public conscience the idea which took root was that Christianity came from Rome and was that what Rome would decide. The resurrected Jesus reigned in Rome and from Rome the Roman Pope was his executor!

Finally, it is necessary to remember another very important factor in this process of the transformation of Rome in the supreme Kingdom of Jesus on earth: the Muslims!!! (Reader, please do not be amazed!) See: starting in the VIII century the Muslims were conquering, one by one, all the great cities of the Near East and the West, which were the headquarters of the first and traditional Christian cities, which may and actually did overshadow Rome, such as Alexandria and the North of Africa (1167), Antioch and Jerusalem (1187), and mainly Constantinople (1453). In those very important cities, the Muslims completely exterminated Christianity. Rome was freed from the conquering fury of the Muslims thanks to two historical battles: 1) in the sea the Battle of Lepanto by John of Austria, October 7, 1571, in front of Naupacto in the west of Greece, 2) in land, the Battle of Kahlenberg to protect Vienna, August 31, 1683, by the King of Poland Jan III Sobieski. These two battles stopped the march of the followers of Islam towards Rome, which was their golden dream.

It is true, Rome was saved from falling to the Muslims but at the same time the Muslim invasion signified the complete destruction of Christianity in the cities which had been the most important in Christendom, and left Rome alone, without any competition. Thus, it was very easy for the bishop of Rome to declare himself the chief and the arbiter of the Christian world.

This was the way in which Rome, which had nothing to do with Jesus Christ, became the center of Christendom and Christianity.

Well, this was the evolution of one of the components of the struggle for power, the part of Peter. And the other component? ... the part of Mary Magdalene and the women? This component was lost in the dust of the centuries .. She was the repentant prostitute ... Wasn't she?

Conclusion to the First Part

As a conclusion for this first part, we can assert without any doubt that the power of the historical Peter was inexistent. The same Gospel of Matthew, which has been used to affirm such a power concludes with a Peter who, after having been an apostate and having denied Jesus, takes off crying bitterly. And nothing else! He simply disappears! Right there, the mentions of Peter completely stop in this important gospel.

As it is evident now, the famous verse *"And I tell you that you are Peter, and on this rock I will build my church, and the gates of Hades will not overcome it. I will give you the keys of the kingdom of heaven; whatever you bind on earth will be bound in heaven, and whatever you loose on earth will be loosed in heaven"* is a bold interpolation, rather blasphemous since it takes away from Jesus his position of the Church cornerstone and gives it to a human. Whoever did it, probably in the fourth century, made a huge and unforgivable mistake but perhaps it was good because it made it easier to demonstrate the adulteration of the biblical text. As it can be seen in the other gospels, there is no such thing as an edification of churches, or gates of Hell, or Kingdom keys. The Gospel of John treats Peter a little bit better since it concludes with his re-incorporation to apostleship after his apostasy.

In reference to his character and personality, judging by all the documents which mention him, Peter is a simple man, analphabet, illiterate, and ignorant, who lives from his work in fishing, an impulsive man, violent at times. Self-determined and "machista", mainly self interested.

Women must obey him to the extent of self-sacrifice to submit to his point of view as can be seen in the case of his paralytic daughter in the Gnostic Gospels. In reference to Mary Magdalene, he does not tolerate that a woman may receive a special communication from

Jesus and simply declares her "crazy" for saying that she had seen the resurrected Jesus.

In reference to his personal feelings, it seems that he was interested in spiritual themes since he immediately accepted his brother's suggestion who invited him to meet Jesus. This is the way that he encountered Jesus and became one of the apostles ... or maybe he did it for personal interest...?

The *Acts of the Apostles* present a Peter who is considerably different from the one portrayed in the Gospels. His three famous speeches alone show a leader with a strong character unafraid of anything. Obviously, he is not the same person.

Here, in this study, we have paid less attention to his person and characteristics in order to discover whether Jesus made him the foundation of any church, or whether he went to Rome with purpose of creating there a religious organization. Of course, nothing of the sort! On the contrary, the same Gospel, Matthew's gospel, which appears as granting Peter such supremacy, ends up with the already quoted text: **he bitterly cried and ran away!** Amazing! He, simply, disappeared.

Nevertheless, the enthronement of the Roman Popes in the name of Peter and through Peter bring Jesus to Rome was a skillful maneuver which allowed that a Satanic power could govern Rome and by means of Rome dominate the world. The history of the Popes demonstrates both aspects. It is important to mention here Saint Paul's text: "Satan disguises himself as an angel of light" (2 Cor. 11:14).

SECOND PART

MARY MAGDALENE

Foreword

The popularity of Mary Magdalene has grown to the point of being omnipresent today. Nevertheless, this woman only appears in the Canonical Gospels in two instances in Jesus´ life, with a total of twelve mentions of her name all together. Of those twelve mentions, only one refers to the daily life of Jesus. The other eleven are related to His death -- seven refer to the cross and the tomb and four to His resurrection.

Compare this scarcity of biblical references with the over two million articles that appear today on Mary Magdalene in electronic search engines, such as Google, Yahoo, Cuil, etc. It could be said that this woman, about whom we know almost nothing, has become a great current theme.

Despite the shortage of biblical quotations regarding Mary Magdalene, her name has the largest number of citations among all the biblical characters after Jesus and his mother. There are fifty-three verses in the New Testament which contain the name of the Virgin Mary, the mother of Jesus, and forty-one for Mary Magdalene, considerably more than the rest of Jesus' disciples and apostles. This fact alone shows her importance above all the women and men in the Bible.

In order to proceed in an organized manner, we will to study all references to Mary as they appear in "the four gospels" also known as "the canonical gospels." Then, we will examine those which are known as the "Gnostic" and/or "Apocryphal" documents. Within these, her name appears in several *Acts of the Apostles*, *Apocalypses*, and *Gospels* from the second and third centuries. A quick look at the early writers of the Christian Church will conclude this study. My only purpose for this effort is offering the readers a comprehensive and total picture of this admirable woman, who gained not only the attention of Jesus, but of the entire civilization of the Western World.

Until recently, there had been references to Mary only in the four gospels, and a few citations in the writings of the Church Fathers. Later, the *Gospel according to Mary* surfaced about a hundred years ago. Now, we enjoy the documents discovered in Nag Hammadi, Egypt, in 1945. From these sources combined, we have a better picture of Mary Magdalene, which does not substantially differ from the original image given to us in the four traditional gospels.

Chapter I

Mary Magdalene in the Canonical Gospels

The Presence of Mary Magdalene in these ancient texts:

a) Passages in reference to Jesus´ life

The first time that the name Mary Magdalene appears in history, occurs possibly between the years 65 and 70, in the first Gospel, the one attributed to Mark. It mentions her in relation to the accounts which refer to Jesus´ death.

There is only one quote which mentions Mary Magdalene during the life of Jesus and it appears in the Gospel of Luke, chapter 8, verses 1 - 3. This very short passage informs that Jesus had organized a vast preaching campaign to announce the Kingdom of God and had walked from city to city and from village to village accompanied by an entourage of twelve men and many women (the Greek text is very clear, it says "pollai = "many"). Luke does not reveal the names of the male companions, nor does he say how many women; however, he specifically mentions three of them: 1) Mary Magdalene, about whom, the evangelist informs the reader that seven demons had gone out from her, 2) Joanna, the wife of the King Herod´s steward, and finally 3) Susanna, about whom no details are given. This passage concludes with the important information that the women maintained Jesus and His companions: *They provided for them out of their own resources* (dihkonoun from diakonew = to provide someone with the means of life).

Tradition has always interpreted the word "Magdalene" as a native of the city of Magdala. This ancient town, located on the northwestern side of the Sea of Galilee, about 120 miles to the north of Jerusalem, used to be an important commercial site during the days of its most prestigious citizen, Mary. Historians mention up to eighty establishments dedicated to the commercialization of fine wool and the textile dyeing process. At the same time, large amounts of money were invested in the exploitation of fisheries. The name given to the town by the vast Greek population living at Magdala was "Tarichae," which means pickled fish.

The name "Mariamne", which appears in the ossuary attributed to Mary Magdalene in a recently discovered tomb in Talpiot, near Jerusalem, is also a Greek word [22]. All of these clues suggest that Mary could have been a member of one of the wealthy Greek families established in Magdala, or perhaps she was the owner of one of those industries, given her enterprising character. Also, the fact that Mary's name is cited in connection with important women, such as the wife of the King's administrator, is quite suggestive of an upper class condition, which --in some way-- may explain Peter's constant rejection of her, being he unrefined and uneducated.

This text of Luke 8: 1-3 presents a rich variety of meaningful circumstances in the life of Jesus. The text asserts that Jesus selected a few strong and dedicated men, although rude and illiterate, to create the initial group of disciples. It also states that He surrounded himself with several affluent and intelligent women, capable of establishing the administrative command and logistics of His apostolic organization.

The fact that Mary Magdalene and the wife of the King's administrator would take charge of maintaining Jesus and his ministry, presupposes that these women had important connections and knew how to administer money. It seems very reasonable that

---

[22] It is very possible that this ossuary is truly the one of Mary Magdalene. If so, it would be evident that she never left Jerusalem and that the story that she traveled to France and became the ancestor of a royal dynasty is only medieval legend without any real basis.

the wife of a man in the royal court could have the means to support Jesus' ministry. On the other hand, regarding Mary Magdalene, only two pieces of information are known: 1) that she came from Magdala, a city of many financial resources and that she economically maintained Jesus. It would not be unreasonable to believe that she was a person of a comfortable financial position, perhaps of Greek origin herself. 2) The second piece of information is that "seven demons had gone out" from her (Luke 8:2). The evangelist does not mention how the seven demons had gone out of Mary, nor what those demons were. The Gospel of Mark adds a bit more to this information; in chapter 16:9 it states that it was Jesus who made the seven demons to go out (ekbeblhkei = to bring out). Both passages, Luke and Mark, mention the exit of demons as the only characterization of this woman. It is obvious, then, that this information is the key for understanding Mary. What does it mean?

First, it is necessary to determine what goes out from her as a result of Jesus´ action. The Greek text uses the words "epta daimonia" = seven demons). This is to say that Jesus took away seven demons from her. In classic Greek, the word "daimonion" (demon) simply meant "god." Thus, we find the term in Socrates' writings in the fifth century BC. In addition, we can read it in Xenophont´s works as a simple synonym for "god." Nevertheless, in the first century, and in the Greek language used by the Jews, the word had evolved and meant simply a "spirit", but a "dirty spirit."

In addition, the interpretation of the number **seven** is needed. This number was and continues to be a symbolic number. It means the perfection of something (there are seven cardinal virtues, seven church sacraments, seven capital sins, God rested on the seventh day after creation, Jesus commanded us to pardon not seven but seventy times seven, etc.). Thus, this number symbolizes absolute human perfection just as the number six means the opposite, the absolute imperfection, as the one who almost arrives but really does not, which is worse than being far off the mark.

According to what has been exposed, the word "seven" applied to "demon" ="dirty spirit" means exactly that, "a **very** dirty spirit", "**perfectly** dirty". In other words, Jesus freed Mary from a very dirty spirit, possibly the dirtiest.

Now we have to find out what was "**extremely dirty**" for Jesus and for the biblical writings. In chapter 6 of Matthew's Gospel, verse 24, Jesus absolutely declared that what opposes God is "mamwna" (mamona) = wealth: "*You cannot serve both God and money*", he emphatically stated. His brother James wrote in reference to the rich: "*Your wealth is rotting (...) your gold and your silver are corroding away*" (James 5: 2-3). Also in Luke 16:13 we read: "*You cannot serve both God and wealth*". Previously, the book of Proverbs in the Old Testament (3:9) said: "*Honor God with what you have*" commanding to commit any wealth to God as the only possible justification of its use. For this reason, Luke 18:25 states: "*it is easier that a rope enters the eye of a needle than for someone rich to enter the Kingdom of Heaven*".

It is clear then that the conversion of Mary Magdalene consisted of switching her money from serving herself to championing God's cause. This is to say, she withdrew her money from luxuries and vanity (the "**dirty** spirit"), and put it towards the **pure** spirit = God's word through Jesus' preaching. All of this coincides with the fact that Jesus did not have a job, nor work of any kind; He only preached the word of God, and Mary's money served God as commanded by the Book of Proverbs. Thus, the "converted" Mary conformed with Jesus' command: "*Do not store up treasures for yourselves on earth ... but in Heaven ... For wherever your treasure is, there will your heart be too.*" (Matthew 6:19-21) Does this not describe Mary Magdalene?

Compare this image of Mary to Pope Gregory's blasphemous and deranged affirmation of her in his sermon (Homily N° 33) preached in the year 591, that declared Mary Magdalene "a mulier in civitate peccatrix" (a woman sinner in the city = a prostitute). As a monk, obsessed with sex, Gregory I interpreted the seven demons as sexual sins. Clearly, Jesus could not even remotely make such an association. Moreover, as Mary was His preferred one among all women, the Papal accusation is not only incompatible with the Biblical account, but also incomprehensible. Regretfully, the Pope's aberrant and absurd slander extended throughout the world up to this day, despite Pope

Paul VI correcting his colleague in 1969 and officially reestablishing Mary Magdalene's honor.

Furthermore, it does not seem possible that Pope Gregory, a Benedictine monk, so refined and educated as they were, and so successful as he was since he had achieved the Papacy, could inadvertently say such a moronic thought. It is more than obvious that he had a hidden intention. Jesus had placed women at the top of his organization as we are seeing in this study. For the monks, who had been slowly taking over the church with the imperial help since the fourth century, women were a problem from any point of view. The American writer, Marcia Ford, quoting Elaine Pagels, affirms that to brand Mary Magdalene as a prostitute was the most adequate instrument to solve the problem of women in the Church. Now, it was possible to say: *"No, she was not a disciple, an evangelist, the companion of Jesus; no, she was a prostitute. This was not only the way to slander women but also to attack their aspiration of assuming positions that, according to a Church Father, were exclusively masculine functions"*. Without the need of going back in history to verify this statement, we can read Pope John Paul II who not long ago said that: *Christ, in His free and divine decision, clearly witnessed by the Gospels and the constant Tradition of the Church, charged the Church ministry only to males. (IV World Women Conference,* Beijing in 1995) **What is interesting here is that both, the Gospels and the Tradition, show just the <u>opposite.</u>**

This concludes the first part of the twelve Biblical quotations in which the name of Mary Magdalene appears, the one which refers to Jesus' daily life. The other eleven quotations pertain to Jesus' last moments, death, tomb, and finally His resurrection.

b) Quotes regarding Jesus' death.

Seven quotations of Mary Magdalene in the gospel of Matthew pertain to the death and entombment of Jesus. Chapter 27 begins with the Jewish priests and elders of the people trying to condemn Jesus. Finally, Pontius Pilate, the Roman Prefect, decrees Jesus' death by crucifixion. In verses 55 and 56, Matthew mentions that the many women who were serving Him during his preaching in Galilee (diakounousai) were now viewing the crucifixion from far away[23].

Matthew mentions three among the many women who had dared to come to the place of the execution; the first one was Mary Magdalene; the other two, were married and mothers. One of them was also named Mary, mother of Jacob and Joseph; and the other woman (no name given) had two sons from her husband Zebedee, James and John.

Regarding the previous passage, note the adjective "many" (pollai) applied to the noun "women" (gynaikes). Today, we are used to seeing many women in churches; however, it was not like this in those days, and it was even less common among Jews, whose women were to remain inside the home. Even worse was the fact that a young female led innumerable women (many of them married) traveling from town to town throughout Galilee, accompanying a man, and were now all in Jerusalem. This had never happened before! It was totally unheard of! In all these texts, we find the same information: Mary Magdalene went ahead of all women.

The gospel of Mark states that after the death of Jesus:" *there were some women watching from a distance. Among them were Mary of Magdala, Mary who was the mother of James the younger and Joset, and Salome. These used to follow Him and look after Him when He was in Galilee. And **many** other women were there who had come up to Jerusalem with Him."* (15:40-41) It is very interesting to realize that both evangelists coincide in underlining "the many women" and the leadership of Mary Magdalene.

In chapter 19, verse 25 of the Gospel according to John, we read something more amazing yet, that Mary Magdalene was not in the distant place mentioned by the previous evangelists. She had moved to the very foot of the cross, close to Jesus' mother who was there with her sister. This daring move exposed her to several dangers and

---

[23] The verb "diakounousai", related to "diekonoun", used by Luke, can both be interpreted as "to maintain". This is to say, that the many women maintained Him.

improper treatment by the soldiers and by other possible enemies of Jesus. This gesture reveals in her a strong character, an admirable decision, and a tremendous love for Jesus.

c) Quotes regarding the tomb and the resurrection

1. References to the tomb:

The third group of passages which mention Mary Magdalene refer to the sepulcher. Matthew tells that a former disciple of Jesus, a rich man from Arimathaea named Joseph, had obtained permission from Roman authorities to take the body of Jesus. He wrapped it in a white sheet and placed it in his own new tomb, which he had excavated in the rock. Joseph then rolled a large stone across the entrance of the tomb and left (Matth. 27: 57-60). The following verse informs that Mary Magdalene and the other Mary were there simply sitting opposite the sepulcher. It is obvious that the brave Mary Magdalene had followed Joseph of Arimathaea to find out what he was doing with the body of her beloved and placed herself there to accompany Him also in death. It is extremely moving to picture her there, crying inconsolably, simply seated, waiting ... Waiting for what?

The gospel of Mark, chapter 15, confirms the above information, and in verse 47 establishes the specific cause of Mary's interest: "*where was He laid*"? The reason for this interest comes right after in chapter 16:1. It reads "*Mary of Magdala, Mary the mother of James, and Salome bought spices with which to go and anoint Him. And very early in the morning of the first day of the week they went to the tomb when the sun had risen*".

Not once do the evangelists take away the primacy of Mary Magdalene, as if they knew that it could not be any other way. On the other hand, the responsibility for the disposal of the body, its anointment, and its allocation in the tomb belonged to the immediate family of the deceased, such as the husband or the wife. In all these passages, Mary Magdalene is described as a leader, a strong person who knows what she wants and undertakes it with firm resolution.

She is also seen in the roll of a caring wife with love guiding all of her efforts.

2. References to the resurrection:

Here we finish reviewing the passages referring to the sepulcher. Now we will study the last four quotations, the ones in reference to the resurrection.

In the gospel of Matthew, the resurrected Jesus appears first to Mary Magdalene, although she is not alone in the passage but accompanied by *"the other Mary"*. (Matth. 28: 1-19). This occurrence begins with the apparition of an angel *"his face was like lightning and his robe white as snow"* (28:3) who announces that Jesus has resurrected and commands His disciples to gather in Galilee where they will see Him. Both women left the sepulcher *"with great joy"* in order to see the disciples. At that moment, Jesus met them and said: *"Greetings"*. The women hurried to Him and paid Him homage. Then, Jesus asked them to announce the good news to the disciples and to inform them that they must go to Galilee where He would meet them (Matth. 28: 1-10). Notice that Jesus does not appear to the apostles, or to the disciples; rather to the women and sends them as His envoys (from "apo" + "stellein" = "to send forth", a messenger, apostle). Thus, the women are the apostles to the apostles. Over the years, Roman Popes have created confusion about this point (see Pope Paul John II on previous pages) in order to maintain male supremacy in the Church. It is important to keep in mind that Jesus did not send the apostles to the women, but instead, the women to the apostles.

The gospel of Mark precisely mentions which one of the two women was the first to see Jesus. In Chapter 16, prior to verse 9, Saint Mark declares with certain emphasis that Jesus appeared **first** to Mary of Magdala, from whom He had cast out seven demons. She ran to the disciples with the information that Jesus was alive and that she had seen Him. Although she was the first witness, the men did not believe her, nor pay her any attention. In the next section of study, the *Gospel According to Mary,* we will see a better picture of Peter and the other disciples.

The Gospel of Luke, asserts that unnamed women, who had been with Him in Galilee, followed Joseph of Arimathaea to see where he had placed the body (Chapter 23). Then, they returned to buy spices and ointments. Chapter 24 begins with the same women who had bought the spices and now go to the tomb in order to anoint the body. There, two men[24] in bright clothing enlighten them about the significance of what they were witnessing, mainly the facts related to the resurrection. The women then understood the importance of the moment and went to tell the apostles and the disciples, who did not believe them. It is interesting to see the disbelief and the lack of cooperation by the males.

The tenth verse of this chapter states: *"The women were Mary of Magdala, Joanna, and Mary the mother of James. And the other women with them also told the apostles, but this story of them seemed pure nonsense, and they did not believe them."*

In this gospel, Jesus does not appear to any women or anyone at all; later, He manifests himself to two male disciples (one of them named Cleopas) who were traveling to Emmaus.

At the tomb, it was not Jesus who appeared to the women, but the two men in bright clothes. They gave the women lessons on exegesis and an interpretation of Jesus' words. As usual, the leadership of Mary Magdalene is unmistakable. She is the first woman to transmit the words of those two men to the rest of the disciples.

Thanks to the Gospel of John, we have the best representation on Mary Magdalene's encounter with Jesus. The information is not only complete, but also extremely moving: *"It was very early on the first day of the week and still dark when Mary of Magdala came to the tomb. She saw that the stone had been moved away from the tomb."* (20:1-18) The chapter begins with Mary Magdalene who subjugated by anguish, was not able to sleep and left her place at dawn to go to the

---

[24] In this gospel, those who instruct the women are two men in brilliant clothes; it does not say "angels".

sepulcher. The Greek text emphasizes it with three phrases: "very early", "first day", "still dark". For a text so short, the fact that the three out of six components were dedicated to the same thing, shows evident emphasis.

Chapter 20 continues with a detailed description of Mary's next steps: she runs to the disciples; in this case to Peter and another one whom Jesus distinguished [25] and tells them that the body was not in the tomb. She was the first witness of the empty tomb. Immediately, the three of them run to the sepulcher. The beloved disciple arrives first, then Peter. Both authenticate the items found in the empty place: linen and a shroud removed from its original place. Having finished this inspection, they returned to the place where the disciples gathered. Mary, on the contrary, remained there crying inconsolably. Despite the evidence that Jesus was not there, she insisted on verifying it: "*Then, as she wept, she stopped to look inside*" (20:11). This is the moment in which the unexpected occurs: two angels, dressed in white, were standing at the exact site in which the body had been placed. To her amazement, one of them asked her why was she crying. Mary's answer revealed her candor and intense love for Jesus: "*because they have taken my Lord away and I do not know where they have put Him*".

The following passage is extremely touching. In the darkness of daybreak, Mary noticed the presence of a stranger who asked her for the reason of her crying. Believing him to be the man in charge of the place, Mary did not answer him directly, but with great naivety asked him another question: "*Sir, if you have taken him away, tell me where you have put him and I will go and remove him*". Amazing! She herself will take Him. Clearly, Mary Magdalene is much more than one of the "many women". In addition, according to Jewish law, to touch a corpse made impure the person who touched it, except for the wife or the husband.

What follows is even more astounding. In the obscurity of the

---

[25] Although no name is given, the tradition has always believed that this beloved disciple was John, the same who supposedly wrote this gospel.

hour, the visitor reveals himself by his voice saying only one word: "*Mary*". How many times He may have said it! With what charm! With what intimacy! to the point that immediately Mary jumped into his arms exclaiming with great emotion: "*Master!*" Jesus answered: "*Do not cling to me because I have not yet ascended to the Father **but go to the brothers and tell them**: I am ascending to my Father and your Father, to my God and your God*".

After having changed the objective of her money and having entrusted her with the financial management of His group, Jesus made her the apostle to the apostles, His delegate, His personal representative. This passage reveals the profound union between Jesus and Mary, represented by their intimate communication, by the inflection of their voices, and the embraces which were not possible then due to the urgency of the moment. Mary fulfilled Jesus' request and brought His message to the disciples.

Thanks to the New Testament's texts previously studied, we know that Mary was the first person who discovered the empty tomb and was the first witness of Jesus' resurrection. In addition, she was also the first apostle- Therefore, we may call her the first Christian, since this is the true meaning of being a Christian -- to affirm the resurrection.

None of the evangelists offer a physical description of Mary Magdalene, or of anyone who populates the pages of the New Testament. We do not know the physical aspect of Jesus, nor that of His clothing. The same can be said for Mary. We know that she managed money and that she put it toward the service of Jesus' preaching campaigns (Luke 8:3). That was her conversion. Perhaps, Mary may have been using her wealth for luxuries or financial investments prior to her conversion. After knowing Jesus, she put whatever she had at His service.

A painting from the 17th century by Alonso del Arco presents her in the act of tearing off her jewels and throwing them far from herself. Perhaps this may be the best representation of Mary Magdalene in the history of art. Regrettably, Alonso del Arco was under Pope Gregory's perverse influence, judging by the licentious attire with which he painted the saint.

We do not know her age, or her physical appearance, or her voice, or the clothing she wore, or her home when she met Jesus. We only know that at a given moment, she began to accompany Him on all of His trips and preaching, in His martyrdom, in His death, and in His resurrection. Since that moment, she never separated herself from Him. For this reason, a famous hymn on her describes her as the "captive spouse".

We may finally affirm that all four gospels present Mary as the faithful love who cannot live without her beloved's presence, as quoted by the hymn: *"At dawn was Mary because she was in love."* Is this not the most wonderful characteristic that we can assert about her?

Another piece of information that we know is that Jesus felt the same for her. All four gospels give her the primacy of Jesus' attention. Specifically, Mark and John testify that Jesus appeared first to her, and to her alone. John added something very important that we cannot overlook. As aforementioned, Peter and John ran to see the tomb that Mary had reported empty. They arrived, looked around, checked every detail, and left. Meanwhile, Jesus remained invisible. As soon as they were gone, Jesus appeared to Mary; to Mary alone, and commissioned her to bring His message to the same Peter and John who were there a few minutes before. We cannot say that Jesus did it because He was a neglectful person. It is obvious that He intentionally did not reveal himself to Peter and John. Moreover, why did Jesus not give his message to them directly when they were there? It is more than obvious that He did not wish to do so and, to the contrary, made Mary Magdalene <u>the</u> apostle to the apostles. This is the glory of Mary.

All characteristics previously mentioned define Mary Magdalene as a person totally disinterested in herself. Her personal interests became vested in her beloved Jesus and His mission. She dedicated her existence to Him without fear of the dangers it signified during the most tragic moments of Jesus' life.

We should not pay any attention to what the misogynists may have said throughout history to conceal or distort this reality, as we have seen before in the case of Pope Gregory the First..

It is necessary to make a pertinent observation here: the gospel of Luke, as previously mentioned, does not present Mary Magdalene or the other women as witnesses of the resurrection. In said gospel, Jesus does not appear to anyone except to two men later, on the road to Emmaus. In addition, if we consider that the Christian tradition believes that the *Acts of the Apostles* was written by the same author, Luke, it is not strange then that this book does not mention the women, nor does refer to Mary Magdalene at all. Maybe this is the beginning of the massive exclusion of women which occurred in Christianity after Jesus' passing.

Keep in mind that "to be a witness of the resurrection" is what makes a person a Christian. For this reason, the gospels of Matthew, Mark, and John make Mary Magdalene the first Christian in history, our most magnificent model through the centuries.

Up to this point, we have studied the primordial importance that Jesus attributed to Mary Magdalene according to the official (canonical) gospels. In the next chapter we shall review other writings of the era, which for different reasons were not included in the official canon and are considered "apocryphal" (apo -kryptein = hidden or secret) [26], among them, the recently discovered "Gnostic" documents ("gnostic" = from knowledge)[27]. In these gospels, Mary

---

[26] Lately, the word apocryphal is being interpreted as "not true". Nevertheless, it is not the meaning of the word, which really means "hidden" or secret. For this reason, we will use the term "apocryphal" here according to the real meaning --secret, not open to the ignorant general public.

[27] There is a great wealth of studies on the Internet pertaining to Gnosticism, including Valentinus and "Valentinian gnosticism". Valentinus was one of the more influent Christian Gnostic teachers of the second century. He founded a movement which expanded to the whole of Europe, the near East and northern Africa. Several documents that we will immediately study are connected with his school in one way or another. At the same time, the Coptic studies are important for the next section.

Magdalene appears more clearly defined. In the canonical gospels, we notice her importance, as we have seen so far, but that importance is not explicitly apparent. The Gnostic gospels paint a clearer picture of Mary and her significance in Jesus' life.

Chapter Two

Mary Magdalene in the Gnostic and apocryphal writings

The "Gnostic gospels" were early accounts of Jesus' teachings, written anonymously during the first centuries of the Christian era, which deviated from the ones officially accepted later. Several of these documents have been recently discovered, saved by fortuitous circumstances from the general burning ordered by the "Proto-orthodox" group. The name "Gnostic" comes from the Greek word "Gnosis" meaning "knowledge", derived from the fundamental principle common to all these groups -- salvation by knowledge.

The most important finding of Gnostic texts occurred on the west coast of the Nile River in December of 1945 at Nag Hammadi, Egypt. Two countrymen, looking for fertilizer, found an amphora which contained thirteen books (codices) consisting of 52 treaties, gospels, acts, and apocalypses, which were not translated or studied until 1977. Other similar documents had been discovered earlier in Egypt, at the end of the 19th century/ beginning of the 20th. For this reason, this study will be divided into two sections: 1) documents before Nag Hammadi (1945) and 2) those of Nag Hammadi as long as Mary Magdalene is mentioned.

Section I: Documents before Nag Hamadi (1945)

I. a) "Gospel according to Mary"

Among the texts discovered in the 19th century, the *"Gospel according to Mary"* is probably the most significant of all, although not all researchers consider it truly Gnostic. This document is of extreme importance in the history of western culture because it is one of the earliest writings that shows the struggle for dislodging women from the preeminent place that Jesus gave them.

So far, three copies of this gospel, in varying degrees of preservation, have been found. Two Greek versions from the end of the 2nd century/ beginning of the 3rd, and one translation into Coptic from the fifth century. All of them were found in Egypt beginning with the Coptic version, which was discovered in 1896. An unknown dealer in antiquities from Cairo sold this very well- kept copy to the German investigator, Karl Reinhardt. It had probably been stolen from a tomb in Akhmin, in the central region of Egypt. Despite its good condition, this volume is missing six initial pages and four center pages. The Greek versions, found in Oxyrhyncus, Egypt, were more deteriorated and published in 1917 and 1983. Today, these documents are kept in three different places: 1) The Coptic version in the Egyptian section of the Museum of Berlin, Codex 8502 Berolinensis, 2) One of the Greek versions, identified as Papyrus Rylands 463, is at John Rylands Library, Manchester, England, and 3) The other Greek version (Papyrus Oxyrhyncus 3225) is in England, at Oxford in the Ashmolean Library[28].

---

[28] For more complete information on this gospel, consult King, Karen L. *The Gospel of Mary of Magdala-Jesus and First Woman Apostle*. Santa Rosa, Ca. Polebridge Press, 2003. This work is the most complete study not only on the Gospel of Mary but in the history of early Christianiuty. Prof. King is in charge of the Ecclesiastical History at the Divinity School, Harvard University. See also Santos-Otero, Aurelio. *Los Evangelios Apócrifos*. Madrid: Biblioteca de Autores Cristianos, 2004. It is also very important to consult the three volumes published by Editorial Trotta in Madrid, *Textos Gnósticos. Biblioteca de Nag Hammadi,* with excellent introductions for each text, by Prof. Antonio Piñero from Universidad Complutense, Madrid; José MonserratsTorrens from Universidad Autónoma de Barcelona; and Prof. Francisco García Bazán from J.F.Kennedy University, Buenos Aires, Argentina.

According to the more complete Coptic version, we may assume that the *"Gospel according to Mary"* would have started with a long speech from Jesus after His resurrection that may have occupied the six initial lost pages. Page seven begins with a question: *"¿Will matter be totally destroyed?* followed by the answer from Jesus: *All nature, all forms all creatures exist each one in itself and at the same time coexist with the others. Each one will separate and dissolve within its own root because it belongs to the essence of matter dissolving in what it is and belongs to its nature.* At this time, Peter intervenes and says: *"You have explained all themes to us; tell us one more thing: What is the sin of the world?* Jesus answered: *Sin as such, does not exist, but rather you are the ones who sin. when act according with idolatry[29]" (pag. 13).* This "idolatry" which appears in this text, and in many other biblical passages under the name of "adultery"[30], should be interpreted as loving things more than loving God, who lives deep inside of each believer. Precisely, this concept agrees with Luke 8: 1-3 as seen before, in reference to Mary Magdalene's conversion: to give up love for material things and to put them towards the love of God's word.

In summary, this gospel develops as follows: 1) After Jesus' death, the disciples and the apostles are reunited with Mary Magdalene. 2) Jesus has resurrected and appears to them. 3) The apostles ask him questions that He answers. 4) Then, Jesus says goodbye and gives them three recommendations: a) keep peace among themselves, b) do not be deceived by those who say that Jesus is here or there because He will always be inside of those who truly look for Him. c) Do not

---

[29] All quotations are transcribed from the Karen L. King's work already cited. The translations are my own following the English version of the *Papyrus Oxyrhyncus* 3525.

[30] See *The Acts of the Apostles,* 15:20 Jesus' brother James was the head of the first group of Christians after Jesus' departure. He supervised the first Christian convention, the Council of Jerusalem. After listening to the different opinions from all disciples regarding the obligations of the new Christians, he concluded that the new Christians were not under the Jewish law; they should only abstain from idolatry and participation at the Idols 'table. That is to say, abandon the idols and their rites and *"God who can read everyone's heart showed His approval of them by giving the Holy Spirit to them just as He had to us".* (Vers. 8) See also Prophet Hosea in the Old Testament, where "adultery" refers to idolatry.

give more commandments than those that He had already given them, and do not establish laws like the legislators.

Then, the Savior bid them farewell and asked again that they keep His peace. The disciples cried inconsolably. Moreover, they feared that if their enemies did not exempt Jesus from death, they would certainly not forgive them either.

From this moment on, Mary was at the center of the meeting and the apostles and the disciples addressed all their questions to her. "Then Mary stood up, greeted them, tenderly kissed them all and said: *"Do not cry, do not be afflicted, do not doubt because His grace will be always with you protecting you. Let's then bless Him because He has reunited us and has made us true human beings."*[31]

When Mary concluded this salutation, the disciples and the apostles began to comment on the Savior's words (page 15). Peter took the initiative and told Mary: *"Mary, sister, we know that the Savior loved you more than any other woman, tell us, then, all what He has told you privately that we do not know"*.

Mary replied that she would teach them all what was still unknown and revealed that the Savior had appeared to her and had congratulated her for not having hesitated in front of Him. Regretfully, the next four pages were lost and with them most of Jesus' revelation to Mary.

Andrew responded and said that he did not believe that Jesus had said all those things. Peter supported Andrew's position saying: *"Is it that we must accept that the Savior secretly spoke to a woman and not openly so that we all could listen to Him? Is she more than us?*

Levi stood up and told Peter: *"Peter, you are always ready to let yourself to be taken by anger. Now, you are confronting a woman as if she were an enemy. If the Savior considered her worthy, how do you dare to despise her. He deeply knew her and loved her more than us. Our duty is then to do what He has commanded us and go out to preach the good news."*

---

[31] Notice the phrase "true human beings" for "true men" and compare with previous texts.

In her commentary to this gospel, Professor Karen L. King underlines the parallelism established between Jesus and Mary: a) Jesus speaks, b) the apostles ask, c) Jesus answers. After Jesus' departure: a) Mary speaks, b) the apostles ask, c) Mary answers.

This gospel is in perfect consonance with the canonical gospel of St. John where Jesus waited at the tomb until Peter and the other disciple left and then, he appeared to Mary and charged her with His mission to the apostles. They preferred not to believe her and considered her insane. Here, in the *Gospel of Mary*, the same thing occurs: Jesus withdraws and Mary takes His place. Peter and Andrew reject her and consider her a liar because only males should be at the top of the Church. That is precisely what happened later on, and Levi's defense was slowly fading into the background and total oblivion.

Another gospel which surfaced in recent years is the Gospel of Thomas; it presents the same situation although worse: Peter declares that *"Mary must leave us because women are not worthy of Life."*

The insistence seen in the *Gospel of Mary*, that the disciples should abstain from giving more commandments beyond the ones given by Jesus, points out the exclusion of women. This tendency, which started right after Jesus' passing and even before, is more visible in the Gnostic gospels. Recall the text of the First Letter of Paul to the Corinthians, chapter 14, verses 34 and 35: *"As in all the churches of God's holy people, women are to remain quiet in the assemblies, since they have no permission to speak; theirs is a subordinate part, as the Law itself says. If there is anything they want to know, they should ask their husbands at home; it is shameful for a woman to speak in the assembly"*. This text is a parallel to Paul's command to Timothy (I Tim. 2: 11-12): *"During instruction a woman should be quiet and respectful. I give no permission for a woman to teach or to have authority over a man. A woman ought to be quiet ..."*

It is of no importance that these texts may not belong to St. Paul. The majority of scholars do not accept that these letters were written by Paul; they belong to the 2ⁿᵈ century, as it is obvious by the more organized ecclesiastic organization that they reveal. At the same time, the verses previously quoted from the letter to the Corinthians, are also late interpolations.

What is important here, is to establish the main purpose of the *Gospel of Mary*: to denounce the progressive abuse against women; a goal clearly fulfilled. Its point of view does not show Jesus as the realization of the Jewish prophecies. According to scholars Karen L. King and Elaine Pagels, this gospel comes from a Greco-Roman background and deals with different questions originating in that environment. It shows the adaptation of Christianity to the stoic and platonic ideas dominating that time and place. In his book Timaeus, Plato had declared that a woman was a deviation from the human ideal. This concept was reproduced in the 13th Century by Saint Thomas Aquino, the origin of all Roman Catholic teachings. In addition, Plato had said that people who fail to achieve the necessary perfection for eternal life, must reincarnate successively in order to achieve purification; they reincarnate in a form appropriated to their characters; people who did not live according to justice, and all cowards reincarnate as women. (p.42)

In summary, we can say that the *Gospel of Mary* recapitulates all these questions in order to affirm the capacity and the legitimacy of women's leadership in the first place, as Jesus did. It is also obvious that the book´s objective is to refute Platonic ideas, which regretfully had invaded Christianity.

To complete this study on the *Gospel of Mary*, it should be said that, in some way, it is similar to the canonical gospel of John, written around the same time. John's gospel is the only one which presents so many anecdotes referring to women, mainly to Mary´s mission as the person selected by Jesus to bring His message to both the apostles and the disciples.

I. b): "The Gospel of Thomas"

Many ancient writers such as Hippolytus of Rome and Kyrillos of Jerusalem, quote a Gospel of Thomas, but not this particular one. There are many texts with similar names, such as The Acts of Thomas, The Pseudo Gospel of Tomas, and the Book of Thomas.

This particular one, *The Gospel of Thomas* must be the oldest known Christian document. In 1898 a very much deteriorated Greek copy was discovered in Oxyrhyncus, Egypt, near the Nile river. According to many scholars, it must have been written by year 50. In 1945 another copy, this one in Coptic language and in better condition appeared among the codices of Nag Hammadi. It is considered a translation of a Greek copy probably from the year 200.

It is not a narration in the typical style of the canonical gospels, but a collection of 114 Jesus' sayings which begin with the phrase: "*Jesus said*". Its title declares: "*These are the secret words that Jesus the Seer pronounced and that Didymus Judas Thomas consigned in writing*". The first of Jesus' saying states: "*Whoever may find the meaning of these words will not taste death*".

It is very interesting to note that "Judas" (according to Mark 6:3) was one of Jesus' brothers and that the additional words ""thomas" and "didymus" mean the same thing, "twin", both in Greek and Aramaic. This coincides with an old tradition which believed that Judas was the twin brother of Jesus.

This gospel is significant for this study because two passages refer to Mary Magdalene. Some sayings found in this gospel are also quoted in the canonical writings, but many are only found here. They are difficult to understand and keep the critics busy. The point of view is different from the one seen in the *Gospel of Mary*, the Greco-Roman world, but one derived from a Judeo/Christian environment. The scholar Aurelio de Santos-Otero believes that this gospel was written for a judeo/Christian community in Syria[32]. The two sentences that will be studied here are numbers 21 and 114, the last one. They are the only ones referring to Mary Magdalene.

Sentence 21 presents a question from Mary to Jesus: "*Marihan said to Jesus: What your disciples resemble to? He answered: They resemble a few boys who have made themselves comfortable in some else's property*".

---

[32] *Los Evangelios Apócrifos*. Madrid: BAC, 2004.

A long explanation follows regarding Jesus' answer. It is very obscure and difficult to understand. What is interesting here is Mary's question. We do not know to what stage of Jesus' preaching these *logia* belong. It seems likely that they are from the very first days. Mary Magdalene already accompanies Him and tries to understand the kind of people that He has selected. The way Mary posed the question is very meaningful, *"What your disciples resemble to?* It obliges Jesus to establish a comparison. Although we do not know the kind of education Mary has received, her question reveals an analytical mind. In addition, it is obvious that she is seriously studying her surroundings.

The last sentence, N° 114, is related to this one. It says: *"Simon Peter told them: "Marihan should leave us because women are not worthy of Life. Jesus said: I will take care of making her a man so that she may become a living spirit, identical to you, men because each woman who becomes a man will enter the Kingdom of Heaven.*(Santos Otero, page 385)

Amazing, but not difficult[33] to understand.

First, we have to return to Sentence N° 22 from this document. While passing by a few children, the apostles asked Jesus whether becoming like children would enable them to enter the Kingdom of Heaven. Jesus' answer is again enigmatic. It reads: *"When you become capable of doing one thing out of two; and configure the interior with the exterior, and the exterior with the interior and what is above with what is down and reduce to unity what is masculine with what is feminine in such a way that the male stops being male and the female, female.*

As we can see, in this gospel like the one of Mary, human perfection consists of synthesis; but synthesis is not possible in life on earth. The body must return to its roots, dust, and then, without the physical part, a human being can be free. To be masculine or feminine is physical and does not belong to the spirit.

In this text Jesus is really saying that he will take care of making

---

[33] See footnote 12 in reference to Peter's character.

her a man, a perfect man[34]. A "perfect human being" (which is the real meaning of the English word "man", derived from the Latin word ""humanus"), a perfect human being far beyond the "masculine/feminine" stage. Possibly, this text refers to the beginning of Jesus' mission right before Mary's conversion, when she may still have been emphasizing her femininity with her money. After her conversion, she had reached perfection by completely consecrating herself to the Word of God in Jesus.

The point to emphasize here, is in sentence 114 of the *Gospel of Thomas*: the resentment and bitterness of the male disciples due to the election of Mary. Remember the passage of Luke 24:11 in which Mary and the other women informed Peter that the tomb was empty and that Jesus was not there. Peter and the apostles bitterly despised the women and called them insane. Furthermore, from the study of chapter 20 in the Gospel of John, it is evident that Peter must have realized that he was being overlooked because of a woman; Jesus waited until he and John had left to appear to Mary and entrust her with His message, a message that essentially said to go to Peter, and the rest of the disciples, to tell them of His will. Why did not Jesus give His message to Peter right there and then? Evidently, Jesus wished to give it to Mary in the first place.

In the Gospel of Mary, Peter reacted terribly when he realized that Jesus had communicated first with a woman. *"Mary must leave"*, declared Peter with wrath. In the *Gospel of Thomas*, we see the results of this reaction: all women must leave from church leadership roles and remain submissive under the males. Thus, it has been done until today. The final corollaries of this study clearly show that the disappearance of women from the high command of the Christian Church was not accidental, but rather a carefully planned procedure, firmly maintained throughout the centuries.

---

[34] Notice that the word "man", from Latin "humanus", and this from "humus"(dust) truly means "from dust", a being made out of dust .

1. c): "The Gospel of Peter"

Bishop Serapion, of Antioch, Syria, said at the end of the 2nd century that he knew of a Christian community that was reading the *Gospel of Peter*. It was also mentioned by other ancient writers up until the fourth century. Nevertheless, no copy of its text could be found until1887. A Greek fragment describing Jesus' death and resurrection according to Peter, was discovered in the tomb of a Christian monk, in Akhmin, Egypt. Scholars believe that this document was written in the year 150[35]. The reason for which it is included in this study is that its sections XII and XIII refer to Mary Magdalene and the women. We do not know whether Peter's animosity towards Mary inspired this gospel. The truth is that Mary's image --although she appears as *"the Lord's disciple"* emerges twisted and scared. More than that, she looks petrified by terror and unworthy. Clearly, this is not the picture of Mary that we know from the Gospel of John and other documents from those days. This presentation of Mary is evidently dominated by the spirit of Peter.

I. d): "Wisdom of Jesus-Christ"

This Gnostic text was discovered by the end of the 19th century together with the *Gospel of Mary*. It was probably written by the end of the second century or beginning the third. Its main concept is that Wisdom rejects the thoughts of the philosophers and glorifies the words of the Lord. It is based on an anecdote from Jesus' life: After His resurrection, Jesus revealed Himself to the disciples in a pure and immaculate flesh as when he appeared to them at the Mount of the Olives[36].

After a short introduction by the narrator, a lively dialogue begins between the Savior and a few disciples. Among them are Phillip, Matthew, Bartholomew, Thomas, and Mary Magdalene, who has

---

[35] This information has been taken from Aurelio de Santos Otero, *Los evangelios apócrifos*. Madrid: BAC, 2004.
[36] Piñero. *Textos Gnósticos*. Vol. II, pag 194.

two entries in the conversation; the first one shows an image of her already known from the previous documents, a practical woman in search of answers. Jesus was explaining the perishable character of matter when Mary interrupted to ask: *"Lord, how can we learn all of this?* As an answer, Jesus referred to the importance of knowing the Father. Mary interrupted for the second time and revealed the same practical capacity and her interest in the disciples as seen before. Mary asks: *"Holy Lord, where do your disciples come from and where will they go and what will they do in that place?* (p. 204). It is extremely difficult to continue since the text is quite deteriorated. In addition, a few pages are missing. Obviously, Mary was referring to the place that Jesus would prepare for those who accepted and loved Him.

I. e): "Pistis - Sophia"

This one must be the most famous of the Gnostic writings. It begins with a strange title *"Faith - Wisdom"*. The copy we have is a Coptic[37] version proceeding from a possible Greek original written on parchment in the fourth century. It was brought to Europe in the 18th century and purchased by the British Museum in 1875.

The book begins with a narration of the fantastic universe in which the Gnostics used to place their speculations. Afterwards, Jesus teaches about the material world and how to escape from it by acquiring the true knowledge. His presentation progresses by means of a series of intelligent questions asked by the disciples, particularly by Mary Magdalene who appears to be much more advanced in spiritual perception, that Jesus interrupts his speech to praise her: *"Blessed Mary, whom I will bring to total perfection with the knowledge of all mysteries from above.* Immediately, Mary declares that Jesus has dominated the malignant powers which control the material world

---

[37] The Coptic Language is the name used to refer to the last stage of the written Egyptian language. Coptic should more correctly be used to refer to the script rather than the language itself. Even though this script was introduced as far back as the 2nd century BC., it is usually applied to the writing of the Egyptian language from the first century AD. to the present day.

and has liberated those who possess the true knowledge, from the rule of Destiny. Jesus enthusiastically replies and praises Mary as *"the most blessed among all women because you will be the plenitude of all plenitudes and the fulfillment of all fulfillments".*

Vis a vis such an extraordinary praise, Peter becomes infuriated and accuses Mary of taking over the interview with the Savior: *"Master, we cannot tolerate this woman who gets always in the middle, does not allow us to participate and continuously talks ".* At once, Mary replies to defend herself and says: *"Master, I believe I have the right to speak at any moment in order to interpret what Pistis-Sophia has said but Peter intimidates me, threatens me and hates women".* Jesus, then, stands-up and declares: *"Anybody filled with the Spirit of Light has the right to stand-up in order to interpret what I say and nobody has the right to prevent it".* Immediately, He congratulated Mary and declared that she had become *"a pure spirit".*

It is obvious that the lesson taught by Jesus is that there is no distinction of sexes and whoever reaches the true Knowledge is a superior being. In this case, Mary is superior than Peter because Peter still makes judgments based on the inferior forms of matter. Mary on the contrary, has reached the plenitude of knowledge, which is the key for the total liberation from matter.[38]

II. Documents from the Nag Hammadi collection (1945)

a) "The Savior's Dialogue"

This book belongs to the first part of the second century, discovered at Nag Hammadi in 1945. It has no missing pages but its preservation is extremely poor. It begins with a Gnostic styled introduction about the final transit of the soul through the celestial spheres and the hostile powers of the Archontes of the Demiurge. After a short exhortation by the Savior about the importance of

---

[38] The information for this section has been taken from *The Secret Books of the Egyptian Gnostics,* by Jean Doresse and from *Peter, Paul, and Mary Magdalene,* by Bart Ehrman.

preparing for the time of dissolution (death), a fast dialogue begins among Jesus and the three favorite disciples for the Gnostics -- Judas (Thomas), Matthew and Mary Magdalene.

The first interrogation by Mary refers to the present reality of being in a body. This point leads Jesus into a theme that the Gospel of Phillip develops: *"Who remains in darkness will not be able to see the light but if someone is not in darkness will not be able to see light"*. The second inquiry by Mary (whose name appears here in the Greek form of "Mariamne") reveals her practical character, as we have seen her before. She asks: *"Where are you going to place the things that you ask the Son of Man?"* Jesus is the one who answers and does so with a typical biblical concept: *"in the heart"*. It is in the heart where these teachings are to be preserved. The third reference to Mary is a praise by the narrator who declares that Mary spoke as a woman who fully understood the truth. Soon after, Mary asks: *"Why do we come to this world -- to suffer or to obtain some benefit? Furthermore, is there a place in which truth is missing?*" Jesus answers that the truth is where His presence is allowed. Mary, recognizing that this is precisely what she has done, exclaims: *"Lord, you are terrible and marvelous!"*

The next inquiry of Mary reveals her other side, her contemplative character. She asks: *"I wish to know all things as they are in themselves."* The Lord's response confirms our interpretation of Mary's conversion as presented in the first part of this study: *"The joy of this world is false. Its gold and its silver are destructive"*. Jesus confirms for her that whoever looks for true life has the true wealth. The dialogue concludes with the Lord's declaration: *"If you have understood all I said, you will be immortal"*. To which Mary answered: *"In this we are"*[39]

---

[39] Piñero and others. *Textos Gnósticos*. Vol II, page 173. Madrid: Editorial Trotta, 1999.

II. b) "First James' Apocalypse"

This book belongs to the group of works attributed to James, the Lord's brother. Its original must have been written in Egypt by the end of the third century[40], addressed to Christians of Jewish origin.

The text coincides with chapter 15 of the canonical book, *Acts of the Apostles* in the New Testament. The younger brother of Jesus, James (Jacob) presides at the Council of Jerusalem, the first Christian meeting. James appears in consultation with Jesus regarding the mission of the twelve male and the seven female disciples. Among the seven women, James gives the name of four, the first being Mary Magdalene. He admires them because *"weak vases have become strong by the presence of the divine action"*.

In a footnote, the authors of the commentary inform the readers that while the Judeo/Christians reduced women to a secondary function, the Gnostics always placed the female in a position equal to the male. Mary Magdalene is always the starting point for the transmission of the Gnosis.

II. c): "The Gospel of Phillip"

We study this gospel last because it is the best document regarding Mary Magdalene among the texts found at Nag Hammadi, in 1945. Scholars believe that the Greek original belongs to the beginnings of Christianity, somewhere in the Second Century. It is impossible to know its author. In section 91, the name of the apostle Phillip is mentioned and the last line brings the title *"Gospel according to Phillip."*

In general, the style of this text is highly symbolic and obscure like the other Gnostic books, a condition which is aggravated by its poor preservation. The scholar, Santos Otero, believes that it was produced by the Gnostics of the Valentinian School.[41]

The name of Mary Magdalene appears for the first time in paragraph 32: *"Three women walked always with the Lord -- His mother*

---

[40] Piñero, idem, Vol. III, p.84.

[41] Santos Otero, page 94.

Mary, her sister, and Mary Magdalene, known as His companion -koinonós; therefore the three of them are "Mary", His mother, her sister, and His companion".

The main theme of this work seems to be the absolute union, by means of the masculine/feminine symbolism, which appears to be descending from the superior realities, such as Christ and the Holy Spirit, the Savior and Holy Sophia, down to Jesus and Mary Magdalene. At this point, the *Gospel of Phillip* reaffirms what has been said before, i.e. *"Jesus' companion is Mary Magdalene"*. The word used here is very clear "companion=koinonós", from the Greek verb "koinonéin" which means "to copulate"; in other words, a complete "companion" including the sexual aspect.

Despite the blanks which this section contains, the scholars believe that the author added the following paragraph in order to explain the previous one: *"The Lord loved Mary more than all the other disciples and kissed her on the mouth.[42] The disciples asked Him the reason for which He loved her more than them. The Savior answered with a question: Why I do not love you as much as I love her?*

The following paragraph, N° 56, seems to explain this mysterious explanation given by the Lord, i.e. that the Lord´s preference is always in proportion to the degree of interior illumination. It declares: *"If a blind person and one who sees are in darkness, there is no difference between the two of them, but when the light arrives, the blind man remains in darkness while the other one sees."* Possibly, it refers to the total illumination by which Mary knew Jesus and her decision to put both her person and her wealth at the total service of the Word of God.

Section III: Apocryphal Documents

By the name of apocryphal" gospels we know certain narratives of Jesus' infancy. They are not very old and lack of credibility. Similar to these, we have a few more gospels that refer to the crucifixion and the resurrection. In addition, there are letters from Nicodemus,

---

[42] The scholars believe that for the Gnostics a kiss on the mouth was a ritual of initiation, as seen in *The Second Apocalypse of James*.

Joseph of Arimathaea, Pontius Pilate, Emperor Tiberius, King Herod, Emperor Vespasian and his son, Titus, etc. These letters are not reliable. Only one is of interest here because it deals with Mary Magdalene. It is a supposed letter from Tiberius to the Prefect Pontius Pilate in which the Emperor tells Pilate that Mary Magdalene has come to Rome and visited him. She declared herself a disciple of Jesus and told the Romans about His miracles and wonderful actions. The Emperor cursed Pontius Pilate and ordered the execution of all of those who intervened in Jesus' death. The letter is significant because it declares the importance of Mary Magdalene in the minds of those first Christians.

There are many more legendary narrations from the fourth and fifth centuries which deal with Jesus still on the cross while his spirit descended to the Underworld full of dragons launching fire. These texts do not deal with Mary Magdalene. Some of them refer to the Virgin Mary and her assumption into Heaven. The apostles have the assistance of a fleet of clouds to go to Ephesus and attend her assumption to Heaven.

IV. Early Testimonies on Mary Magdalene

We do not have many mentions of Mary Magdalene among the early writers of the Church, although a few of them are worthy to note. Saint Hyppolytus (170-236) described her as "*the apostle to the apostles*" in his commentaries on the *Song of Songs*.

Saint Jerome (347-420) wrote:

> "*...Those unbelievers who read me may perhaps smile to find me lingering over the praises of weak woman. But if they recall how holy women attended our Lord and Savior and ministered to him of their own substance, and how the three Marys stood before the cross, and particularly how Mary of Magdala, called "of the tower" because of her earnestness and ardent faith, was privileged to see the rising Christ even before the apostles, they will convict*

*themselves of pride rather than me of folly, who judge
virtue not by the sex but by the mind...."*

The Eastern Christian Church has always taught that she was
a holy woman, and that the seven demons tormented her for this.
She was the first evangelist; having preached Christ's Resurrection
to His Apostles.

Conclusions and Corollaries

Here we conclude this brief review of the earliest historical testimonies on Mary Magdalene. It does not matter that the Gnostic and the apocryphal gospels or any other related records are not canonical or official documents of any church. This study does not deal with religious beliefs of church interests. It is a historical investigation. What can be said of an individual witnessed by more accounts than those which affirm many others accepted by history?

All these documents coincide in asserting her extraordinary character and remarkable personality, as well as her significant role by Jesus' side. These writings also attest to her unique mission as the first apostle of Christianity, and -consequently- the privilege of being the first Christian in history. The professor of New Testament at North Carolina University, Bart Ehrman, goes so far as to call her "the founder of Christianity."[43]

We also pointed out the exclusion that she, and all women, suffered at the beginning of the Christian era. This rejection, perpetrated at the top of the Church hierarchy, mainly in the Roman Church, was intentionally planned by the male members who took over the control of Christianity until today, despite all discourses used to disguise it.

Thanks to the examined texts, we have discovered the firm and constant attitude of Mary to understand the meaning of real Christian living, not only as an individual, but also as a member of the community.

Particularly in the Gnostic texts, we have seen that even in the presence of Jesus, the male disciples (Peter and Andrew) were determined to exclude Mary Magdalene and all women. In the New

---

[43] *Peter, Paul, and Mary Magdalene.* New York: Oxford University Press. 2006, page 229.

Testament, mainly in the letters attributed to Peter, and in the book of Acts, Mary Magdalene and the other women are totally silenced. Peter remembers the women only to say: *"You wives should be obedient to your husbands ... your adornment should be not an exterior one of braided hair or gold jewelry or fine clothing ... submissive to their husbands like Sarah was obedient to Abraham, and called him her Lord". (I Peter 3:1-6).*

In Saint Paul's, there are two conflicting opinions regarding women:

1) In his letter to the Romans, Paul says that he works with women in the Christian endeavors and enthusiastically salutes them:

   "I commend to you our sister Phoebe, a deaconess of the church at Cenchreae (...) My greetings to Prisca and Aquila, my fellow workers in Christ Jesus. (...) and my greetings at the church in their house (...) Greetings to Mary who worked hard for you. (...) Greetings to those outstanding apostles, Andronicus and Junia ...to Tryphaena and Tryphosa who work hard in the Lord ... to Julia, Nereus and his sister... (Romans 16: 1-15). Notice that he gave Junia the title of "apostle".

2) The same St. Paul (although, obviously cannot be the same person) takes a different position in his first letter to the Corinthians. In chapter 14, he emphatically declares:

   "Women are to remain quiet in the assemblies, since they have no permission to speak: theirs is a subordinate part, as the Law itself says. If there is anything they want to know, they should ask their husbands at home; it is shameful that a woman speaks in the assembly".(14: 34-35)

In the following chapter of the same letter, this Paul completely erases Mary Magdalene and the Gospels' statements which we have previously studied by affirming that, after His resurrection, Jesus: "*appeared to Cephas (Peter) and later to the twelve and next He appeared to more than five hundred brothers at the same time. (...) then He appeared to James, and then to all the apostles. Last of all, He appeared to me ...*" Evidently, they are all males; Mary Magdalene and all women were completely excluded and carefully erased (15: 5-8).

In the first letter to Timothy, chapter 2:11-15, this Paul mandates that "*During instruction, a woman should be quiet and respectful. I give no permission for a woman to teach or to have authority over a man. A woman ought to be quiet.*" He admits that a woman may attain salvation, "*nevertheless she will be saved by child-bearing* (I Tim. 2:15).

In the letter to Titus, he adds: "Subjected to their husbands" (chapter 2:5). In the first letter to the Corinthians (7:4), he reinforces his mandate "*The wife does not have authority over her own body; but the husband does*".

Generally, in the New Testament (except the Gospels), women disappear completely, with the exception of receiving reprimands, prohibitions, and insults as we have seen in the previous passages.

With them, Mary Magdalene is also buried in the obscurity of history, to reappear by the actions of artists and famous painters who, seduced by Pope Gregory's slander, did not resist the attraction and enchantment of the naked body of the "prostitute saint."

Thanks to the persistence of art, Mary Magdalene has reached the modern age and impresses the sensibility of the XX Century. With this, the curiosity of researchers has been awakened. Women have felt the need and the obligation to demand restitution of Mary's honor as one of their own who had been intentionally confined to an adjective (ex-prostitute), which did not belong to her.

After all that has been said, it seems sufficient to conclude this work right here. Nevertheless, it is not finished. The most serious betrayal against Jesus is the one perpetrated by the church of Rome. In addition to taking over the world, according to the model of the Roman Empire, not only did they forbid women to occupy the place assigned to them by Jesus, but added insult to injury by prohibiting women to marry a priest, despite the New Testament order which stated that all church ministers should be married as proof that they were able to manage the church (I Tim.3: 2-5 and Titus 1: 6-8). The nonsense with which they pretend to cover up and justify this violation of God's commandment has caused regrettable damage to Christianity.

In reality, the only reason which they have had for this absurd prohibition has always been the same: woman's essential indignity declared by misogynous males who enthroned themselves where there should be no thrones.

It is no surprise that Church hierarchs like to quote the famous text that someone like them introduced in the book of *Revelation,* in the New Testament. The text refers to the winners in the final battle against Satan, at the end of the world: *"These are the sons who have kept their virginity and not been defiled with women* "(Revelation 14:4).

Amazing, but this is exactly what the Greek original text emphatically and defiantly declares: = they did not defile themselves with women because they are virgins (emolynzesan = to get filthy, to defile oneself).[44]

Particularly now, when the Supreme Roman Hierarchy has declared that a woman's aspiration to minister the altar is one the greatest sins, it is opportune to ask for the whereabouts of one of most relevant biblical mandates: *"There can be neither male nor female -- for you are all one in Christ Jesus"* (Galatians 3:28).

It is unnecessary to mention in this conclusion that the distance between Jesus' attitude toward women --mainly towards His beloved above all others, Mary Magdalene-- and what the Roman Hierarchy did against women is simply abysmal. In addition, the consequences of such actions are even worse --being the cause, as they are, of many, if not all the aberrations of today's Western culture. Perhaps, the more infamous among these aberrations is having brought sex to the

---

[44] The translation is mine. Notice, by the way, how the biblical texts are distorted at the translator's pleasure: *The Holy Bible* (New International Version of 1999) translates the Greek word "gynaikon" = women, as "sexual rites" ? "They did not tarnish themselves with sexual rites". (???) No comments!

summit of human concern for morality. I do not recall having ever been asked in a confession whether I had given a piece of bread to a hungry person (Luke 11:41), but rather, whether I had entertained "bad thoughts" (meaning sex) or had I done those "bad actions" (meaning sex). I do not remember having heard a sermon regarding the meaning of true religion as protecting the orphans or the widows as it is mandated by the New Testament (James 1:27).

Only by understanding this subversion of values is it that we can comprehend the injustices and aggressions that History reveals among peoples who declared and still declare themselves Christian. -- wars, invasions, torture, and the mass killing of those persons who did not agree with the Hierarch of the time. Think of the despoliation of the Americas blessed by Popes and bishops, a plunder, pillage and exploitation so huge and enormous that is not easily visible. A Spanish Pope, Alexander VI (his real name: Rodrigo Borgia) dared to make a gift of the Americas to "the Catholic Kings" without even for a moment thinking that those lands belonged to their rightful owners and that the wives and daughters of those "Indians" were not public women for the service of dissolute and licentious conquerors blessed by the Popes. This is the true original sin of the American continent. With it, we were born --true original sin which perpetuates itself like a "domino" effect until today, still not capable of freeing ourselves from the original vortex -- rich countries which are poor because wealth does always "belong" to the powerful ruler at the time; all of it crowned by a dull education based on meaningless and pointless prudishness, essentially an obvious, but invisible sin of omission.

In addition, the industry of religious images and statues has sent to the human masses a silent and regrettable message: a sexless Jesus Christ, son of an asexual woman, surrounded by infinite saints, male and female, virgins as if the essence of Christian life and salvation was a sacred "abstinence", in a church which lives with its back to the majority of the inhabitants of this planet who struggle with hunger and disease each day of their lives.

The repercussion that a recent novel -- The Da Vinci Code -- had at the high religious spheres, made evident this sad reality: a Jesus married to Mary Magdalene raised the unanimous clamor of every bishop: *"Blasphemy!!!!"* as if sex were not a creation of God, the essential characteristic of the whole creation, particularly of human beings, mainly the most authentic human being who is supposed to be Jesus and His preferred one among all women, Mary Magdalene.

In the Festivity of Saint Mary Magdalene, July 22, 2012

Bibliography

Boer, Esther de. *María Magdalena más allá del mito*. Buenos Aires: Lumen, 2004.

Carter, James. *Textos apócrifos del Nuevo Testamento*. Málaga: Ed. Sirio, 2006.

Crossan, John D. *The Historical Jesus*. San Francisco: Harper Collins, 1991.

Davis, J. G. *The Early Christian Church*. New York: Barnes & Noble Books, 1995.

Doresse, Jean. *The Secret Books of the Egyptian Gnostics*. N.Y MJF Books, 1986.

Ehrman, Bart D. *Jesus, interrupted*. New York: Harper One, 2009.

_____*The Orthodox Corruption of Scripture*. Oxford Univ. Press, 1993.

_____*Peter, Paul, & Mary Magdalene*. Oxford: Oxford Univ. Press, 2006.

_____*Lost Christianities*. Oxford: Oxford University Press, 2003.

_____*Lost Scriptures*. Oxford: Oxford University Press, 2003.

Filoramo, Giovanni. *A History of Gnosticism*. Cambridge, MA: Blackwell, 1990.

Giménez José. *El legado de María Magdalena*. Zaragoza, España: Interactiva, 2005.

Hureaux, Roland. *Jesús y María Magdalena*. Madrid: Iberica Graphic, S.A., 2005.

Jacobovici, Simcha and Pellegrino. *The Jesus Family Tomb*. San Fco: Harper, 2007.

Kelly, John. *Early Christian Doctrines*. San Francisco: Harper Collins, 1978.

King, Karen. *The Gospel of Mary of Magdala - Jesus and the First Woman Apostle*.

Santa Rosa, California: Polebridge Press, 2003.

Leloup, Jean-Yves. *El evangelio de Felipe*. Madrid: Arca de Sabiduría, 2004.

Meyer, Marvin. *The Secret Tradition of Mary Magdalene, the Companion of Jesus*. San Francisco: Harper, 2004.

Pagels, Elaine. *The Gnostic Gospels*. N.Y. : Vintage Books, Random House, 1979.

Piñero, Antonio, et all. *Textos Gnósticos*. Madrid: Editorial Trotta, 2000.

Pomeroy, Sarah B. *Goddesses,Whores, Wives, and Slaves. Woman in Classical Antiquity*. New York: Random Press, 1990.

Ranke Heinemann, Uta. *Eunucos por el Reino de los Cielos*. Madrid: Editorial Trotta, 1994.

Reina-Valera. *La Santa Biblia*. Buenos Aires: Sociedades Bíblicas en América Latina, 1960.

Santos Otero, Aurelio de. *Los evangelios apócrifos*. Madrid:B.A.C., 2004.

Starbird, Margaret. *Magdalene's Lost Legacy*. Rochester VT: Bear & Co. 2003.

_____ *Mary Magdalene, Bride in Exile*. Rochester, Vt. : Bear and Company, 2005.

Wellborn, Amy. *Descodificando a María Magdalena*. Madrid: Ediciones Palabra, 2006.

Printed in the United States
By Bookmasters